PUBLICATION
APR 4

HANDBOOK

OF REASON

DAGOBERT D. RUNES

HANDBOOK
OF REASON

PHILOSOPHICAL LIBRARY
New York

1741440

Raise not your children in disdain of Israel; I say unto you, take out the venom from your Scripture so that my people may live!

D. D. R.

INSTEAD OF A PREFACE

The one and only Pope ever to speak out in behalf of the Jews, Pope John XXIII before his death had composed a *Prayer of Repentance* in which this true vicar of Christ begged God's forgiveness for the untold suffering brought upon the Jewish nation by the members of the Catholic Church. On his deathbed the Pontiff urged that this prayer be said in all Catholic places of worship. Up to now, this has not been done; the good Pope's wish should be neglected no longer.

Quoting from Pope John's *Prayer of Repentance:*

> *"We admit that over hundreds of years our eyes were blinded, so as not to see the Beauty of Thy Chosen People and not to recognize the features of our firstborn brother. We admit that the sign of Cain is upon our forehead. For centuries Abel was lying in blood and tears while we had forgotten Thy love. Forgive us, O Lord, the curse we unjustly spoke out over the people of Israel. Forgive us, that in their flesh we crucified You the second time! We did not know what we were doing. . . ."*

ABSTRACT

Art of old, sometimes siding with the good by drawing, sculpting, and painting ennobling themes, sometimes siding with the devil by glorifying conquering dictators—art has deserted both the angels and the devils for no one in particular. It just vanished into the abstract, nonobjective night of unrecognizable splotches on canvas, rules and dots and cubes, seen through a rock with a hole in the middle.

The savage who failed at music fell to beating drums; the painter whose brush fumbled jumped at "nonobjective" scraping or abstract paint-dripping; the musician sans harmony hailed dissonances; the sculptor with five thumbs on each hand delighted in "molding" crazy rocks or senseless metal ding-dangs. In short, the losers won the game.

It is amazing to read emphatic and concise "reviews" of nonobjective "paintings" or "sculptures" by presumptuously didactic critics who have as little idea what the erratic brush work or chisel-chipping means as the cynical "artists" themselves. Much noise about nothing; we live in an era where farmers get paid for not planting and painters for not painting. Only the totally incompetent need apply, since a mere shade of talent would disqualify the participant.

There is, however, a side alley open to the cunning: gimmickry like dripping paint on the floor or magnifying a pebble or painting with one's own mop of hair or with an untidy brush, and the like. For the contemporary reckless pseudo-achiever, there are practically no restrictions on artistic chicanery and bluffmanship. Paint a whole wall brown or throw a brown drop on a white wall, just so the "critics" can have some hook on which to hang their multi-adjectives. They too are in this for the same reason as those on whom

9

they lavish their belabored syntax. What a six-year-old would hide in embarrassment, they help sell for good money to frightened old ladies who wish to be *avant-garde*.

ACHIEVEMENT

Achievement lies not in becoming a bigger man but in making this a better world, not in what you do for yourself but in what you do for the people. Look at Alexander, Caesar, Napoleon, Hitler, Stalin—they crowned themselves with fame and power, yet in one snuff of nature, all was blown to nothing except the million murdered bodies. I have seen the sword of Alexander, the crown of Napoleon and the pipe of Stalin. They all, even under glass, bear the stench of rotting flesh.

What price power! And what shame to build monuments to such monsters!

ADULATION

Adulation is gilding. The Romans were masters at it. That's why we rarely see a Caesar's bust without a garland in his hair (a sow's head with a rose in its jaw). In our day, we have had no shortage of poets and romancers weaving wreaths about the brows of current political monsters—and quiet flows the Don.

AGNOSTICS

Men who think never fail to hesitate and wonder. Only fools and drunks speak of the great and ultimate things with arrogant absolutism. Whatever we know is only a tiny thread in the eternal web of wisdom. We are all agnostics—yet we believe, we hope, we search.

AMBITION

Spinoza reckoned historic ambition among the great failings of mortal man. The fame-greedy would step over mountains of corpses, betray friends and family, desecrate the holiness of life, just to gain the vainglory of historic eminence. They crave for lands not because they need or even want them, just for the glitter of living on in history as conquerors. At the end no one possesses more than a tiny lot of land: three by six.

History vanity is at the root of a thousand wars and a thousand massacres. The conquerors in history pretend to fight for a cause. Deceivers they are, all! Their banners carry slogans of self-sacrifice and devotion but in their hearts is nothing but personal greed for historic fame.

What a price to pay for vanity!

AMERICAN DEMOCRACY

American democracy may have its imperfections, yet no man ever deserted its shores and found a better form of government elsewhere—not because we have the best *civitas;* rather, all others without exception are worse.

AMERICANS

Americans are gluttons for self-criticism. They stage huge rallies because a demented assassin is put away but raise not an outcry if Russia ships any and all opponents to Siberian jails or China decapitates them in the public market-place.

ANTHROPOLOGISTS

Some anthropologists enjoy pontificating from a peak position. They take an old Gibraltar monkey jaw and solemnly swear this is the missing link a million years old and to-

11

morrow they uncover a caved-in skull and that they assure us with vigor is the long-searched-for αυζsoπos. Hesitance is the road to science; impressing the ignorant may bring one closer to success but not to the truth.

ANTI-SEMITISM

Anti-Semitism is a particular parasite. It has infected and still does infect some of the best growth in nature. Augustinus, Voltaire, Luther, Herder, Hegel, Marx, Proudhon —they reached out to the heavens; yet they were all infested with the rot of Jew-hate. Their tongues babbled with words of love, but suddenly they would swing about and snarl epithets of bloody hate against a people that never touched or hurt them.

"Burn the homes and Talmuds of the Jews!" bellowed Luther. "Keep the Jews as slaves forever," sermonized Saint (!) Augustinus. "Exterminate this race like vermin," said "gentle" Herder. And Shakespeare, who never saw a Jew in his whole life, branded them with the sign of usury.

What a pack of vicious wolves those Christian reformers be!

APPEASEMENT

You can't pacify despots, you can only disarm them. A crocodile is harmless only when its teeth are out.

ARGUMENT

Usually arguments are not originated by those who present them but by one or a few who are hidden behind the speakers or writers. Stalin set a million tongues and pens in vivid motion; they spoke as if from a personal conviction while indeed they were only mouthing his. And the very next day when Stalin decided to drop his anti-Nazism and join Hitler as ally in war against Poland, to supply him with weapons, fuel and food, most of the million defenders of Stalin's anti-

Nazism turned into protagonists of Stalin's pro-Hitlerism. All this, as quick as the new line could reach them.

Rare are the people who present and defend their own arguments; as a rule they are no more than mouthpieces for a distant schemer or ideologue.

ASTROLOGY

Astrology has been assiduously practiced by learned astronomers. Thus Learning is no obstacle to the cultivation of most absurd superstitions.

ATHEISTS

If this world exists, then God exists. If I exist, God exists—unless I assume that nothing is nowhere. If this universe of galaxies developed out of a bag of gases, no matter; somebody put the bag here. The rest is silence.

I know not what is beyond the billion galaxies. I know not what or who put the bag there. And those who say they know, they know less, because they don't even know that they don't know. No two people have the same God. No two people think God alike. But we know there is more—much more, a billion years more, aeons more—than we know. So let us be hesitant, and wonder and search.

Saying a meaningless word like atheist means nothing. There remains this infinite universe with infinite attributes and infinite modi of existence. And an ocean of mysteries in the air, in the distances, in the far unknown. So let us search and seek and wonder and have humility in our ignorance. It is so little we know.

AVARICE

Avarice is one of the three mainstreams of desire tossing man's ship of life away from the straight course of personal well-being, the other two being Ambition and Lust.

Such is the philosophy of Spinoza, the sage of Amsterdam. Spinoza reasoned that if man by concentration and deep insight learned to comprehend the vanity of honors bestowed, the dangers of submission to libidinousness and the destructive results of greed, he would raise the horizon of his thinking to the high level of eternal concepts and endeavor to see Creative Nature in its harmonious glory. The deep pleasure and satisfaction that accompanies such intuition, seeing all *sub specie aeternitatis,* would make man forego the petty pleasures accompanying erratically an existence given to greed, ambition and lust. The great joy of living in the light of reason makes the pleasures of disturbing bodily affectations fade into the background; man is no longer tossed about by the Tempting Three and serenely leads a free life.

Spinoza's Free Man is decidedly an ethical individual, since he in his wisdom of the Infinite understands the great causal laws of the universe and therefore hates no person, a mere mode of Nature, nor does he love any thing or creature except in an intellectual form or manner, as he loves God, or to say it clearer, Creative Nature. Free man is dedicated to this *amor Dei intellectualis* in which he finds all things and all creatures in their proper causality. He understands the enemy as he accepts the friend; he is cognizant of hate as he is of love, of rancor as he is of generosity, of envy as he is of brotherhood, of patricide as he is of self-sacrifice. They are all manifestations of Great God Nature and have to be perceived not individually as most people do, but universally, cosmically. Free man thinks the Cosmos, lives the Cosmos, enjoys this Cosmic Vision, and is little perturbed by the turmoil of specific events. To him they are neither good nor bad, neither baleful nor lovable. The Free Man loves his enemy as he does his most devoted friend, as phenomena of Nature, and he would as little strike an offender as he would hit back at a chair; he would as little caress a benefactor as he would pat a flower for giving off sweet scent.

In a deeper sense, however, Spinoza's Free Man is ethical. By freeing himself from all hate and animosity, he would not hurt people by design or deceive them on purpose or seduce them to vulgarity or evil. The Free Man may live in a world of delusion, in a tower of emotional isolation, but to whatever degree his resignation is guided by intuitive insight, he will do no wrong to others. That is eminently important in an era when the learned demonstrate little difference from the illiterate or uneducated in their attitudes and actions toward the downtrodden, the disinherited, and the deprived of our communities.

BENEVOLENT DESPOTS

There is an old Sephardic saying: the Devil keeps a clean house. Among the great oppressors of mankind, past and present, there were quite a few whose windows are well-dressed. Louis XIV of France, who bragged that not a single year of his reign passed without bloodshed, swaggered over the corpses of the villagers of France with royal indolence—yet he assembled at his stupendous palace artists, scholars and literati whose presence is supposed to balance his historical account. Catherine, Czarina of all the Russias, debaucher of peasant boys, and destroyer of whatever trace of freedom Czar Peter left the Russian workers and artisans—the lady conqueror and hangman was a woman of letters and corresponded with the "liberals" of her time. Napoleon sponsored a code of law named after him; Hitler supported youth organizations named after him; Alexander founded cities named after him; Stalin did the same. Mao replaced the Analects of Confucius with his personal quotations; Caesar became his own war correspondent (guess who is the hero?). All of these butchers were responsible for the massacre of millions of children and women. There seems to be an ancient code that men in uniform have the right to kill. All these and other despots have done some "good" here and there. Some built roads—for easier defense; others built schools to train administrative clerks or military experts. Many went to church—exchange visits I suppose to the high clergy for their blessings of the troops.

Let not the gracious left hand fool you; the right behind the back is bloody from the last massacre.

16

BEST SELLERS

Some books sell in quantity; others in depth. The New Testament is the all-time best seller. Look at the world and see for yourself what little effect it had on mankind. Marx's *Das Kapital* was distributed by the millions over the last hundred years.

Christians and Communists read the books, but they acted upon the orders of their organizational masters. By their deeds you shall recognize them, not by the literature they read.

BIOGRAPHY

There are too many books about persons that in reality divulge more of the biographer than the biographed.

BLESSINGS

Blessings of the Church have often in history of the western world been solemnly bestowed on very prosaic, even distasteful occasions. In 1939 there were poised in Germany dominated by Hitler's unholy spirit three armies, one on the east, one on the west, and one in the capital of the Third Reich. Before the armies there stood ten thousand men of the cloth, men who ate the bread of the Christian churches. Each of these clergymen had at his hip a makeshift altar with a shiny cross on top, a reminder of the eternal Jew as hangman and executioner of God's Son.

The clergyman stood there to bless the armies of Hitler, poised to fall upon their neighbors to the east and their neighbors to the west and equally, if not more important, upon the kinfolk of Jesus—men, women and children, all unarmed, unaware of their impending doom, spread throughout the towns and villages of Europe, a Europe that traditionally and by religious training [The Jew is a Son of the Devil and does his father's lust—John viii.44] would never, but never, stand by a member of that race. They worshipped Jesus, adored His mother, but hated their Holy Family's relatives.

These ten thousand clergymen looked up to the Heavenly Father and in somber, prayerful voices invoked success upon the weapons of Nazism, cannon, bullets and poison gas. It seems the Lord hearkened to their prayers because the Nazi armies defeated not only the west and the east but also gassed all the Jews of Europe. If I had faith in the power of prayer like an evangelist, I would consider the good Lord a silly old soul swayed by ten thousand German churchmen of the Christian religion. But I don't reckon that God was persuaded by any priests or ministers or even bishops to tip the balance in any warfare. The Nazis won for a while, then they lost against both the east and the west.

But against the Jews, they won. Excepting some of the Jewish partisans who managed to escape, all of Europe's Jews, women, children and old men, were choked to death with noxious gasses. To give it a special degree of brutality, the Germans placed the children in the execution chambers together with their mothers so they might watch the slow death of their offspring.

It is possible for Russian Christians and French Christians who came out of this holocaust hurt and diminished, yet alive, to continue the hereditary belief in divine providence. For the Jews of Europe, divine providence was a mere chimera, the nightmare of a corpse. The Jew of Europe was not a sick man, not a suffering man—the Jew of Europe was dead. Dead men have no religious convictions.

For the Jew on other continents, with the death of Europe's Jews, God also died. The God of righteousness, of justice and protection had failed. The God of the Christian priests and ministers who blessed Hitler's hordes with the sign of the cross remained an acceptable symbol of celestial providence, a bit jaded perhaps, but Christian Europe was alive. Only the Jews were dead, obliterated.

It is difficult, most difficult, to trust in divine providence when your little children choke to death in twelve tortured

18

minutes before your very eyes and then you yourself feel the devil grip your throat and you pass into nothing. Can there be faith in heaven when all its gates are closed and your anguished voice is hurled back at you by a storm trooper's jeer?

Europe's Christians—in France, in Hungary, in Poland, in the Ukraine—vied with each other to deliver to the gas chambers of Germany all, and no fewer than all, of the Israelites, women, children and feeble old men.

Some of Europe's Christians demanded a price: five dollars. That was what they got for Anne Frank. But most of Europe's Christians did the denouncing and apprehending for nothing, for the mere satisfaction of it. They remembered their gospel lesson: the Jew is the Son of the Devil and does his father's work. The never-dying-out apologists for Christian calumny have a few names of humane Europeans who saved a few of the doomed. The few prove only that you *could* be humane, if such was your nature. But the other half-billion Christians lived their lives in the spirit of Saint John's gospel teaching: the Jews are Sons of the Devil. *Der Jude verrecke!*

The Vicar of Christ gave a warning to all: We Christians will remain neutral and not create doubts in the hearts of Germany's faithful fighting men. We Christians will not protest against the killing of Jewish women and children. We are neutral. Thus spake Pius XII, the Pontiff. How prophetic the exclamation of Nietzsche's Zarathustra: God is dead! It is not Hitler who killed God, but the churches of Christ, in their blessing of Nazi soldiers, in their gospel hate of Israel, in their refusal to lend a helping hand or even a *helping* word to a million children, in their turning away from the monstrous choking of a million young throats.

The Vatican gave Wagner festivals to Hitler's elite in Rome; Protestant bishops placed swastikas beside the altar of Jeshu ben Joseph, the Messiah of Israel. How many of Jeshu's kinfolk, how many descendants of his apostles died in the holocaust we shall never know. But with the little bodies of Israel's children, there on the flaming stoves of Europe's concentration camps died God the Redeemer.

And when the Germans and Ukrainians stopped the hearts of thirty thousand Jewish women and old men at Babi Yar and piled the bodies neatly like logs of wood, there they also buried the testament of Jesus into which the Christian church fathers already had driven one hundred sharp spikes of the ugliest and vilest accusations against Jesus' own people. The Ukrainians, Hitler's willing helpers; the Christians of Europe, indolent bystanders of history's greatest bloodbath—together they made Babi Yar into a garbage heap for the whole pompous Christian theology and liturgy.

What holiness is there in a book of faith that carries within its chapters a hundred malevolent sentences against a people whence God chose his only Son? What holiness is there in a book of faith that teaches its readers from childhood to manhood to disdain the Jews as evil personified? What holiness is there in a book of faith that has Jesus, the Son of Joseph, the Son of David, call his own nation a devil's brood? Jesus never spoke thus of his father's people or his mother's people. The churches that call themselves Christian may have had cynical reason to denigrate the Jew for all time—or was it jealous madness?—but until they expunge from the Christian Bible all malevolent Jew-baiting, it will remain a book of calumny, not a book of holiness.

BOOKS

Books are like apples: some are good, some are hard, and some are just rotten. Heine once complained bitterly about the good Lord's "carelessness" in making the instrument of Love also a vehicle for expelling impurities of the body. On this note, I should like to register my displeasure to whoever invented the Book, that this greatest of all depositories of wisdom, contemplation, history and science is being abused by pushers of filth, perversion and downright printed boredom.

20

Books have in certain civilizations been considered depositories for wisdom. Wise or bewildered, their authors filled them lovingly. We unearth them in caves or graves; they speak to us from millennia gone by of their yearnings, their standards, their spiritual guideposts. The books of death, the books of life, they were then mileposts of man's reaching toward the far horizon.

What are books today? Some are only documentary evidence of a pretentious but generally accepted fraud upon the public, ghostwritten papers put out under the byline of a successful politician, military man or publicity-seeking personality. Some of these nebulous "authors" never even read the books they allegedly wrote. A few self-promoters keep their own writer as a person of wealth would keep a valet or travel companion.

Some books are no more than a wreath of onanistic fantasies held together by a flimsy thread of alleged fiction with four-letter words recurring regularly to give the only semblance of natural cohesion. And venerable literati, lightly bribed and respectfully corrupted, lend their reputation to the noisy approval of this new generation of shock-esque. Juveniles in the underpaid book reviewer's chair bolster the merits of this genital-romanticism grown fat on porno-commercialism. Guys writing this sort of stuff used to avoid looking you in the face only a generation ago; today their pictures stare at you from the front pages of the gazettes and the bookseller's display window.

The world has always had bordello writing; there is nothing new or revealing in it. Astonishing only is the circumstance that the pimps and hucksters no longer lurk in the dark alleys, but sit in the front row of school and society.

The great masses of printed volumes are rather an impediment than a help in education. More than a hundred thousand books are yearly published in the western world: novels and tales, biased and ghostwritten political essays, superficial narratives about cities and people of the past, the present, and ah! the future, psychological observations of tests perpetrated

21

on rats and guinea pigs, on fish and insects, from which college graduates gain a little bit of useless data wrapped in another degree.

A hole in the world should be if a book is missing; I don't think a pinprick of light would show if the very most of them disappeared this instant! Why do so many write so much, especially those who have nothing to say? One man puts together a hundred science fables, another man twice as many detective fictions. And the pens of those doctoral and other academic aspirants. And those politicians who keep a stable of ghosts. Right now the sex analysts and other crotch spelunkers pour out their findings in unending streams. In all this mess, how is a serious student to find the writer who matters and the book that counts? How few, how very few, are the *books* among the millions of printed pages!

BULLFIGHTING

Bullfighting is a euphemistic expression for the slow torturous killing of a dumb animal cleverly coached for months prior to the event in making direct runs toward a red cloth.

What normal person would permit even a child to stick barbed darts into a calf or cat and then chase the bleeding animal to exhaustion? Bullfighting is no more than such brutal exercise.

This and similar shows, like setting two cocks against each other with razor blades tied to their spurs, are mere throwbacks to the glory that was Rome, when wild animals were set against helpless people. Now wild people are set against helpless beasts.

BYNAMES

European royalty used to delight in affixing to their names an elevating cognomen such as Richard "the Lion-Hearted"; Augustus "the Strong"; Charles "the Great"; Maximilian "the Just." We find a similar predilection among the American

22

Indians, who endowed their braves with surnames like "the great hunter," "the quick-tongued," "the killer of wolves." We trust that the Indians deserved their sobriquets more than Elizabeth the Virgin Queen, Catherine the Great, or Mary the Pious.

BYWAYS

If you want the truth in philosophy, you have to search for her in byways and side tracks. The grand avenues of philosophical exposition are full of empty sound and thunder. The thinkers of any time speak not freely in their official parade tracts. What they really mean you will uncover if you read their diaries, letters, notes and footnotes.

CAESAR'S PORTION

In the Roman version of the Gospels there is a saying attributed to the gentle Jew Jesus by Roman scribes: Render unto Caesar that which is Caesar's. Well, there was nothing that was Caesar's in Judea; there was nothing that was Caesar's in Israel. Caesar, whether Vespasian, Titus or Gaius Julius, all Caesars from Augustus to Nero and thenceforth were demons of destruction who attacked all beauty, wisdom and humanity from the Jordan to Jaffa. There was nothing that was Caesar's in Jerusalem or Nazareth. Jesus, the noble Jew, would never preach a slave's sermon of tribute to the savage Roman enemies of God and man. These lines of servitude are put onto the tongue of Jesus, the incorruptible son of Israel, by Constantine's Roman bishops to sap the spirit of the rebels in the Holy Land. This is not Jesus speaking, but Flavian lackeys.

Render nothing unto Caesar, nothing but the naked sword!

CAPITAL PUNISHMENT

Capital punishment is not a pretty thought; neither is capital crime. Countless voices were raised in the free world against the hanging of lust-monsters and assassins, yet only a whisper against the executioners of millions of citizens in Russia and China.

Doing butchery to the body of an alleged or real offender is an old custom. In antiquity and even the medieval centuries, long incarcerations were rare except as waiting periods for trial. Punishment was swift, since the authorities did not care

24

to assume the burden of feeding prisoners for any length of time. People in England of Henry VIII's time were emasculated for treason; in Italy of the dark era, gouging out of eyes was practiced; in Arabic countries, the cutting off of arms; in India, cutting off of noses.

Punishment, even banishment, has its place, but the executioner's block signifies not law but revenge. A murder in haste, a murder in jealousy, a murder in desperate greed, a murder in alcohol or drug stupor, a murder in sex insanity, a murder in calculation by a depraved mind—they are none of them squared by a murder in court.

CASTLES AND DUNGEONS

When you visit a castle, forget not the dungeon. In the palaces you will note how the nobility of Europe treated itself to all the comforts of life, the delicate pleasures to delight the eye, the ear and all the other senses. In the dungeons you will discover how the nobility treated its opponents, its breadmakers, its artisans, its common people, its serfs and bondsmen. The common people of most of the centuries prior to the great revolutions in America and France lived in stinking huts and shacks. When they rebelled they found themselves in icy dungeons in the company of lice and rats.

When you tour the Colosseum, step down from Caesar's gallery, way down to the dungeons where conquered people, freedom-loving people, waited their turn to be fed to the African beasts. Stare not in admiration at the glory that was Rome. Rome's glory was the misery of its defeated neighbors. There are two sides to the coin of civilization. Turn over the laurel-framed profile of the tyrant and from the other side will stare at you the face of desperate misery and deprivation.

When you visit the castles of Europe, spend not all your time in the princely throne room or the gallery of the ancestral statues and paintings; nay, step down to the dungeon, the quarters of the freedom-loving and oppressed, lest the evils of the past overtake the future.

CELIBACY

The demand of celibacy among priests and monks stemmed from sociological rather than sexual considerations. The Old Testament frowned upon celibacy: the Synoptics in the New Testament do not espouse it. Paul, however, encouraged it in expectation of the end of the world, though Peter and all other Apostles may have lived in marital bliss. The Pastoral Epistles required the bishops to be exemplary family heads. At the Council of Nicaea the demand for celibacy was rejected. However, as the centuries passed, it seemed practical to Popes Leo IX (1049-54) and Innocent II (1139) to prohibit priest marriages. But it was only at the Council of Trent (1545-1563) that celibacy was rigidly imposed upon all those taking a monastic vow.

The causes of such measures are apparent, especially relating to the major orders. Monks or nuns dedicating themselves to a devotional existence not only would be personally distracted but would interfere through their families with the insular or monastic life of the cloistered community. Families of monks were found to interfere seriously with the discipline of the orders.

To a lesser degree, this held good for the priesthood. Frequently confessors hesitated to divulge intimacies to family-priests and as early as 343 at the Synod of Gangra, churchgoers were threatened with anathema if they refused to confess to a married priest. Yet another factor in the movement for celibacy was the widespread transfer of church positions from married clergy to their sons (Decretal of 1139, Synod in Rome, Gregory VII).

While these sociological considerations played their part in a thousand-year-long growth of the Catholic Church, somehow in the vestries, in the schools, in the streets and in the homes of the laity, the growing Vatican emphasis on celibacy

26

took the form of derogating sexual intercourse in general. Celibacy, or absence of marriage, became confused with sexual abstinence. Slowly but definitely, Christian Europe, and later the Americas, sank into a morass of biological prejudice, making sexual abstinence a virtue and sexual activity except for the purpose of procreation a sin—in some countries and states, a crime.

Nothing of course could be further from the truth. Sexual activity of adults who are not restricted by marriage vows is a purely personal affair, as are their other preoccupations. Even the breach of a marriage vow is only of concern to the respective couple, no one else. Even if we were to accept Kant's definition of marriage as a contract for exclusive sexual intercourse, a contract is a private agreement among the individual parties to it. Neither the state nor the community has the authority to interfere unless called upon by one or both of the parties. This holds for marriage like any other contract. The state or community should have no right to arrest or indict a person "caught" in breaking a marriage vow and no right to raid hotels or apartments to ascertain such a breach, as they have no right to raid offices or warehouses, plants or laboratories to find evidence of a person breaking a business agreement. And certainly no authorities should have the privilege of interfering with the sex life of adult participants unwed, unloved or divorced, provided such activities occur in the privacy of a home or hotel.

The concept of priestly celibacy, grossly misunderstood in the form of abstinence as a *summum bonum,* has even crept into legislation, stamping thousands of innocent persons as offenders. Incidentally, these "criminals" apprehended in occasional raids by zealous police officers in some of the bluenose states represent only a fraction of the great army of offenders. If our authorities were really willing and capable of arresting all persons who have ever engaged in sexual practice with other than their married spouse, there would be very few left above their teens who might justly escape indictment.

I certainly do not advocate promiscuity, but just state the

above facts to establish the fact of nonmarried sexuality. It may often be in bad taste and muddled by emotionalism, but sex per se is no crime even as abstinence per se is no virtue. What men or women do with their bodies is their own affair. If they are careless with them, slovenly, they will undoubtedly, in my thinking, impair their health, mental and physical. Some participants may claim that they only flourish by such activity. Moralizing will not stop them but often stamps them as what they are not: offenders, criminals. As far as society is concerned, they are neither good nor evil. If there is any harm in what they are doing, it is their concern and there might perhaps be equal harm in the state of abstinence.

Sexuality, like any other biological pursuit, is a matter of hygiene, not ethics. As long as the participants do not directly harm others, they are only living out the tendencies of their lives in a freedom granted them by enlightened society, without fear and without abuse. The flagwavers of abstinence may be self-repressing or frigid or impotent. There is no social virtue in clamoring for all-around conformism. Again, I do not find promiscuity in good taste but I consider moralizing an overemphasis on trivial matters.

The evil in the world is not done by those who fornicate but by hateful and hate-spreading vicious little men who as often as not have their sex under control but not their gall. Hitler lived in almost perfect abstinence; murderous Philip II of Spain, who forbade victims of the Inquisition the little privilege of being garroted before being slowly burned alive ("so they may feel the full wrath of God"), never practiced sex except for procreation and died covered with holy amulets and missal in hand. One can do an awful lot of evil and have a spotless sex life; and one can burn up with the stings of desire and still do good for the rest of the world.

CENSORSHIP

For those who live in the free countries such as the United States of America, England, France, Israel, the Scandinavian countries, Holland, Switzerland, it should be of great significance that two-thirds of the world lives in imposed silence. Persons in Russia, China, Poland, and all the other despotic states are relegated to intellectual silence. They may safely speak, write or print only meaningless little nothings or parrot directives from the authorities. The tragedy lies not only in the existence of such a sad state of affairs, but also that so few, so frighteningly few, rise up with the courage to challenge this muzzling of free citizens. Yet comparatively many in the free countries find it opportune to attack the conditions there without even a courtesy reference to the spiked muzzles of the so-called communist countries.

What makes them wear those blinders and how do they acquire them? Are fellow-travelers just out for the fun of it, having their sport with the masses? Do they really care nothing about anybody? Let's be grateful for those who think and call it as they see it.

CEREMONIAL

Religion means "binding." In far too many, faith is no more than a garland of ceremonies. The Hebrews call it *Shelshelot Ha-Kabbalah,* the chain of tradition. While religious tradition may be expressed in symbolism, it often escapes priests and worshippers alike that only living humanism gives reality to otherwise meaningless links with a religious past.

CHAIRMAN

The Communist presidents and ministers are like Roman consuls: they harangue the plebs and hail Party Chairman Caesar.

CHEERFULNESS

Cheerfulness is neither a sign of wisdom nor goodness. I would rather say that cheerfulness in this century or any century of the Christian dominance is an indication of indolence, not sagacity.

CHILDREN OF CAIN

The Lord Himself asked of Cain, "Where is Abel?" The Christian world did not ask Hitler, "Where is the Jew?" The German Christians did not ask, because five million of them belonged to military and police organizations that did the killing. The French Christians under Pétain sent all the Jews of France including war veterans and infants in sealed cattle cars to German extermination camps. The Pope of the Italian Christians turned away from the window when German agents dragged Jewish women and children from the nearby Jewish ghetto. The head of the Christians of Slovakia, Father Tiso, sold Jewish youths to Himmler for so much a head. The Polish Christians helped the German army to isolate the Jews of Warsaw. The Ukrainian Christians raised a huge army under General Vlasov for the Third Reich and were the enthusiastic associates of the Nazis!

And the Red Cross societies of Europe and America, who have spent months and years to investigate alleged maltreatment of Arabs in Israeli prison camps, the Red Cross couldn't find any suffering Jews in Nazi Europe; they just couldn't find them. They should be named the Blood-Red Cross. While Israel's children were choked to death and Jewish women decimated and the corpses Babi Yar-ed, the Red Cross was giving out sandwiches and coffee to German prisoners of war in Canada.

Only God cried out: "Cain, where is thy brother Abel?"

CHILIASM

Chiliasm, the vision of the Messiah's advent accompanied by final judgment of all, the living and the dead, is a frantic quest by despairing souls for redemption. The hope for a reign of the Messiah instead of a rigid system, secular or ecclesiastic, has been often the spark inflaming millenarian superstitions. The early Judaeo-Christians under the Roman yoke hoped for a Messiah to take them back to Jerusalem, a belief still firmly held by Orthodox Jewry.

Considerable is the number of great Christian and Hebrew scholars of the Middle Ages and Renaissance who upheld chiliastic prophecies. Comenius was one of the many so taken in. In his case as in some others, the yearning for a Good Life was at the root of blind faith, the Good Life in a bitter world. Chiliasts, Christian and Hebrew alike, are known to have sold their homes and left their places of work to start on the trek toward Jerusalem. Some of them hurried, believing that if they missed the advent of the Messiah, they would have to roll on the ground all the way to the Holy Land.

What fools mortals can be, learned or naïve, or both! Millennialism has no moral value, even if it had reality as basis instead of superstition. The chiliast was giving up his worldly goods to gain a top seat in a celestial *Neuland,* not to help his fellow man.

CHOSEN PEOPLE

The Vatican has decided as a phase of its ecumenic gesture to declare the Lord's reference to the Jews as His people, chosen and select, to be obsolete. The new chosen people by papal bull are to be the members of the Mother Church. Since the Pope's utterances are by the articles upholding his office sacrosanct and infallible, there can be no doubt in the eyes of the Catholics that the Jews are now déclassé and the pew occupants of the Church are replacing them as a sort of new aristocracy of Jehovah.

Why God in His days honored the Jews no one will ever know. The Good Book, however, relates that the Jews were tested time and time again for their virtue, sagacity and willingness to sacrifice everything from son to soul, from Abraham to Job. Yet the good Catholics take over all that divine selection by just sitting in their pews!

Hitler declared the Jews an inferior race and chose as the Olympians of mankind not Einstein, not Spinoza, not Ehrlich, but the solid Aryans—Goering, a debauched drug fiend, Himmler, a sadistic voyeur of the gas chamber and Streicher, a well-known pornographer. Those in the pews and those at the torture rack may be inflated by their own magnificence, but all this tinselly grandeur of willful pretense will fall into dust as the mills of time grind on while the Chosen People of the Lord go about their task and quietly harbor in their hearts the word and the commandments of Jehovah.

CHRIST

Christ as He appears in some of the pages of the gospels—disregarding a drift of Jew-hating interpolations—is a magnificent preacher for a revived Judaism. Christ called for a life given to charity (the old Hebrew *tzadaka*), to sharing the wealth with the poor, to respect for the lowly and the stranger, to upholding tradition yet tempering its severity with forgiveness. Yet what has Christianity done with Christ's teachings? As the Christian Church attained power in the third and fourth centuries, it started a vicious campaign against the kinfolk of Christ as being crucifiers of God and burned synagogues and Hebrew schools of learning. The Christians sent out missionaries across the whole Roman empire to teach not Christ's devotion, but their own hate against Israel. The Church not only tolerated slavery but reduced by word and deed all Jews to enslavement. Saint Augustinus, Saint Thomas, every one of the Church fathers and Church theologians demanded that Jews, all Jews, be treated as slaves, property of the sovereign.

The early Hebrew assembly of Christ had faith and devotion. What is the Church today?

It is not Christ on the cross in the New Testament; it is the Living Jew condemned by a Roman theology to be perennially crucified for something He had never done. Our grandchildren and children today are maligned as God-killers by a Bible infested with maliciously interpolated invective designed to create and perpetuate hate against our people for millennia, forever!

The New Testament—they call it a book of love, yet in one hundred and two passages it is a brazen trumpeter of hate against the sons and daughters of Israel, the very kin of Jesus, the gentle Jew of Nazareth.

CHRISTIAN CHARITY

At a glance, it is obvious that the contribution of the Christian churches to the alleviation of human suffering is nearly nil. Slaves in antiquity were admonished by the Catholic theologian Saint Augustinus to be glad of their miserable fate, since being without property, privileges and rights, they were closest to salvation.

In the struggle for abolition of slavery and serfdom in the west of Europe as well as the east, the Christian churches were at best only bystanders. The same of course applies to the Americas. The slaves and serfs were finally freed, not because of the church but rather in spite of the church. The rebels and abolitionists were anything but friendly to the church, as the church was in alliance with the slaveholding establishment, even when the lords of the manor went so far as to demand rights of sexual abuse of all brides in their realm. *Jus primae noctis,* the right to the first night, was either ignored or supported by the Christian church.

The inquisition into the faith of Jews and heretics was also upheld by the Church as was their bestial punishment by spike, prong and torch. The churches did have their own struggles, involving such issues as the nature of the host being flesh of Jesus (bread) or blood of Jesus (wine), celibacy, the confessional, baptism and so on. But never did the Church as such, the Christian Church, struggle for the right of man to be free or for the right of alien religionists such as Jews, Gypsies, Saracens and other "heathens" even to live.

In the days of Hitler, the Protestant clergymen of Prussia almost to a man hailed the Führer, as did the priests of Bavaria. And the then Pope, Pius XII of unholy memory, not once, not even once raised his voice to stop the gassing of a million Jewish children, the poisoning of a hundred thousand Gypsy children. I do not know if God was deaf during the Hitler era; I do know, however, that the Pope was.

CHRISTIANITY

Christianity in its time has known over one thousand different denominations that have attacked each other with words, swords and the torch. Christianity is a brand of religion that was always ready to stab, burn and otherwise torture its dissidents. I wonder if Jesus, had He foreseen the holocaust of two thousand years over four continents, would have wanted His name connected with these bloody twists of "faith." The path of the "heretics" was strewn with persecution, misery and bodily suffering. What price true faith?

And those vast aggregations of professional defenders of the dominant doctrine, the priests, ministers, deacons and monks! From the third century on the fiery spikes of theological torture masters were never permitted to cool. The torches of "correct" doctrine never ceased their agonizing activity. *Sancta bestialitas! Sancta inhumanitas! Ubi misericordia?*

CHRISTIAN LOVE

When the German troops with the help of French police under Pétain and other Quisling forces arrested more than a million Jewish children and struck the little ones' cheeks, the children, who all had attended Christian schools, would have offered the other cheek, but the Germans struck them dead. It appears that admonitions of the Gospels never worked too well, especially not for the Jewish people. The Gospels preach: Love thine enemy. The Germans killed three million "enemies" who shared the Jewish faith in Poland. That is hardly an act of love! The Gospels teach: Thou shalt not kill. Yet the Germans killed six million European Jews by choking them to death in huge gas abattoirs. And the rest of Europe's Christians interfered in only one way; they made sure no Jew escaped. What a sad book the New Testament is, and it was written by Jews! What irony! What blasphemy! They gassed the children of Jesus and all His kin! And they did not even bury them. Six million souls of Israel wandering through the night! *Stille Nacht, Heilige Nacht!*

CHRISTIAN THEOLOGY

1741440

Marxism adopted anti-Semitism as a fundamental passion intrinsic to its thesis. To church fathers who worked on the structure of Christian theology for four hundred years, teaching about Jesus as the all-loving all-forgiving Son of God appeared weak, sentimental. They knew that only hate is given the all-convincing power of conquest and only hate endures. So the church fathers put hate, a specific hate against a specific people, the Jews, into the text. They built into the legend a tortuous drama about gentle Jesus and a whole nation of killers, the Jews, and the plot worked! No one knows who, if anyone, killed Jesus, an unknown carpenter in the Philistine (Palestine) lands of southern Syria; except rumor had it that the Roman procurator's office crucified another Jewish political prisoner. Nothing else is known. But the church fathers needed hate, revenge, blood, punishment forever and ever, and they got it ten-million-fold. They placed the seed of hate, and still do, in every Christian man, woman, and child: "Revenge on the Jews. They killed our God, our Jesus. They must be punished forever and ever. Christ's blood upon the Children of Israel."

This Christian message of hate has brought a harvest of massacre for two thousand years. Ten million defenseless

Jewish persons, among them two million children, were tortured to death by Church and State in all the Christian nations in all continents, and by Christian nations only, excepting only the United States of America. I don't know what wonders Christian love worked, but Christian hate brought forth oceans of spilled Jewish blood, mountains of Jewish bones broken on the rack, ravines like Babi Yar filled with bodies of children and trainloads of naked Jewish women for the delectation of dirty Christian eyes and dirty Christian genitals. The New Testament is the most effective book in existence. Show me one other book that can instigate the killing of ten million people—and all that by a contrived drama of hate.

But those who cherish this testament of hate are not finished, far from it. They still scheme and plan to obliterate the "killers of their kinsman from Nazareth." They are plotting carefully; they might not even do it themselves. They might just hire the executioner and give him the ax. After all, they are Christians, and they do have a reputation to uphold.

The Christians are again on the kill; they never stopped. They have their quarrels, true enough, but by catechism the Jew is damned and they like him to die quietly, be it in the Ukraine, or under the missiles of the Russian air force.

CIVILIZATION

Civilization must be judged not only by the arts it produced but more by its style of human coexistence. The Renaissance brought forth thousands of magnificent paintings and sculptures and musical serenades. Yet the very same Renaissance public enjoyed with abandon the most revolting spectacles of torture of the innocents, the Jews and the heretics. The churches, from St. Peter's in Rome to the chapel in the Spanish countryside, vied with each other for the possession of holy pictures that still adorn them or are showpieces in modern museums. Yet the priests of the very same illustrious era watched with amazing eagerness a Jewish child being burned at the stake or a Jewish woman having her breasts cut with glowing tongs. The centuries of scholasticism in all their subtle scholarship from St. Augustine to Thomas Aquinas declared the Jew—every Jew, every single Jew, man, woman or child—a pariah, a born slave, a predestined property of the sovereign.

The Vatican inspired crusades century after century to save and recoup endangered (*sic!*) shrines of early Christianity in Palestine. On these crusades thousands of Jewish homes were sacked, their powerless inhabitants slaughtered, children decapitated facing their parents and parents cut to death facing their children. And Christian Europe cheered the roving bands of lust-intoxicated riffraff, their greedy knightly nobility and the accompanying men of the cloth. When these more than fourteen separate armies reached Jerusalem, they found no trace of Jesus but hundreds of his unarmed kin. Once the crusaders of Roman Christianity drove the Hebrews into the Great Synagogue and burned them alive. Christian Europe watched indifferently as the Queen and King of Spain with the blessing of the participating Pope ended the Holy Inquisition by burning nine thousand Marrano Jews on the scaffolds of Madrid. This was done to rob them of their property and position. The blood of tortured Israel is not only upon the heads of the unsavory twosome on the throne of Spain, but equally on all of Christian Europe that traveled occasionally to Renaissance Spain not to restrain the savagery of the Iberian clergy and court, but to watch the burning of the God-killers. You can still see the place and traces of the scaffolds erected by the Defenders of the Faith.

When you hear or read or travel, look not only upon the noble paintings; remember the reverse side. You may see the ghostly faces of Hebrew mothers watching in their own agony the pain of dying by fire in the countenance of their children. Perhaps through the sweet tinkling of Renaissance airs you may hear the outcry of the plagued souls of Israel, from among whom the Lord chose to name His Son.

Remember the years of mansions and Lords,
   Of Bishops and Dukes and Marshals and Knights,
When palaces rose on rivers and lakes
   And blanketed wagons brought statues and vases
And paintings and objects and ornaments too.
   What culture, what richness of songs
And ballads and hymns and missals!
   The Past of glory, the Past of the Great and their finesse!
Yet stop and linger. Linger; descend;
   Descend to the bottom, the bottom of glory,
The bottom of art and artifacts.
   Descend to the dungeons, the black,
Bleak roundsteps will take you there,
   There where the rivers and lakes
Nightly caress the sunken walls.
   You can see the chains, the broken chains
Still gripping bony wrist and bony
   Ankles of prisoners of glory.
They died in darkened graves
   Underneath the princely mansions.

They died on the block, on the rack, on the torch, on the hanging links, in the Iron Maiden, bleeding a slow death from the nails in her heart. Remember when you stroll through the palaces and churches, eyes glued on the paintings and statues stacked up to the rafters, that there is a cellar to the art. Descend and see the other side of beauteous culture; see the grimace of the peasants, the serfs, the Jews, and the Gypsies who perished groaning below while the nobles savored the perfumed words and poems above. See the other side of old and ancient culture, the side of the people.

CLERGYMEN

Clergymen sometimes become so deeply entangled in precepts, rituals and theological thickets that they lose track of the Good Lord, who is after all only one and alone and unencumbered.

COEXISTENCE

When tyrants fail, they plead for coexistence; when they are successful, they rule it out.

COLOR

Color as a segregating element among nations is far from being endemic to the western continent nor is it an outgrowth of modern racial theories. It is rather a traditional pattern stemming from a one-time disquieting relationship of supremacy of one color group over another. In India, for instance, the custom of segregation stems from the ancient conquest of the dark Dravidians by the white-skinned Aryans. The victors imposed on their subject natives the principle of *varna* (color, caste). The supremacy of the Brahman castes as custodians of the sacred religious texts was part of the protective establishment sponsored by the victorious warrior families. While the very same establishment fixed the place in society of their citizens by the accident of birth, it was only the dark Untouchables who were radically discriminated against professionally, socially and religiously. The jobs assigned to the Hindu Untouchables bear a striking similarity to the work distribution among the Negroes of our southern states. In India too, the "blacks" (Untouchables) are assigned certain menial tasks, are excluded from the houses of worship of the white castes, are prohibited from entering schools, eating places, parks, beaches, train compartments, theaters and festivals reserved for the higher castes. In the

United States, this sad color segregation was similarly inaugurated by the dominant white groups buying or hijacking blacks from the plains or forests of Africa. This direct or circumspect robbery of black people continued illegally in the United States until the year 1861, when the indictment and execution of slave trader Captain Gordon under President Lincoln made an end to this felonious practice.

There is nothing innate in man's soul which regards persons of black color as inferiors. Color prejudice of the reprehensible variety is historically founded in military superiority and egotistical ruthlessness of lighter-skinned conquerors. There were times when black men dominated white territories and we find there, too, oppressive overbearance by the victors. The dark Carthaginians at times extended their military and economic influence deep into Sardinia and Sicily and the available records indicate that there were places in European antiquity where the color white was low on the spectrum of appreciation. The golden era of Moorish dominance in Granada was on the other hand a meaningful example of a darker nation's tolerance, even generosity, towards its white neighbors. Under Ferdinand and Isabella, however, the tables were turned on the Moors and within the next few centuries, the victorious monarchs of Spain not only reduced the Moors to secondary citizens but slowly and systematically exterminated all of the darker folk, Moslems and converts, Moors and Moriscos alike.

That the Blacks are capable of great cultural achievements is hardly necessary to emphasize. When the Teutons, the Rurics, the Picts, Gauls and Celts were still roaming the forests hunting for game and berries, the Egyptians, the Semitic Carthaginians, the Ethiopians were erecting libraries and temples, fostering sciences and setting forth teachings of lasting import; almost all of this was destroyed by Roman conquerors and roving Vandals of the white race. There were in the Eurasian past dark centuries when the torch of learning had completely slipped away from the hands of the West to be carried by Arabs and Persians, Chinese and Syrians. The light of learning and reverence shone almost alone over the far lands of the East, the yellow, brown and black East, while the white West was given over to the sanguine games of wars and religious persecutions. This is not said in an effort to place the black or yellow man *above* the white, but squarely alongside.

COLUMBUS DAY

Let's not forget America was discovered by men who considered the earth flat and all people except Catholics expendable. Columbus, like Pizarro and most of his ilk, was not a discoverer but a marauder who sailed to the lands of "savages" to rob them, not to save them. These discoverers carried patents and contracts with them assuring them of large shares of the expected loot to be turned over to the kings of Spain and Portugal.

The kings of the Aztecs and Incas were massacred as were the Indian chiefs. Their gold and gems and women were taken as were later on their fields and forests. In later years the grasping kings of Spain and Portugal were overthrown by the natives and their leaders, but the souls of the ravished will never come back nor will their blood that reddened the rivers of the Americas.

There should be no celebration on Columbus Day and similar events on the calendar, but rather rituals of mourning in a visible effort to atone for the many atrocities perpetrated on the ancient nations of the Americas. Let the monuments be erected not to the European robber barons and conquistadors but to the noble memory of the massacred princes of the continent.

COMMUNISM

Communism thus far, after half a century, has presented us not with a better life, but with better promises. Communism has not increased the earnings of the worker, only his subservience. Thus Communism begins with a promise and ends with a promise; in between there is pure despotism.

CONFESSED CRIMINALS

Confessions of guilt score a perfect ten out of ten with two organizations: the obsolete Inquisition Corporation of the medieval church and the Soviet criminal courts. Even their methods of pretrial "investigations" and public "admissions" are identical.

CONFESSION

Confession is good not for the soul but for the sinner. Confession in secrecy before a powerless clergyman is a rather cheap price to pay for an evil deed. The medieval German mass killer, Count Rindfleisch, dragged a worn-out little monk along with his murderous band for daily confessionals, no less. Other "nobles" of old placed special chapels in their castles for spiritual whitewash. They pacified their own muddled consciences, never the ire of the Lord.

During the Hitler era twenty million German Catholics, predominantly Bavarians, participated in the most reprehensible atrocities perpetrated on Jewish and Gypsy children and women. Yet there is not a single record of any of these criminals against civilian populations ever going to confession to lay bare his black soul for possible redemption. There is, however, evidence of an unaltered weekly activity before the confessional curtains of German priests: streams of German servant girls regretting their sins of having toyed with the boss's son, or the boss himself; grave violations of the meatless Friday; a wife's tearful admission of having taken ten marks from her husband's trousers, and the like. The German nation was so profoundly perverted that banal trivia were churched up to "sins" while the sins of Cain out on the bloody skin of Christ's own people were played down by the Vatican itself as matters of military obedience.

CONGRESS

A congress of parliamentary councillors is less a concentration of wisdom than a dispersal of it.

CONNIVERS

The melancholy truth is that the world and its people are not run by persons who think, but by persons who connive. Contrary to Plato's vision, the real rulers are not the philosophers, but rather the schemers. In the democracies, such as the United States, England, France or Italy, at times intellect may appear on top: in the communist and fascist countries, the political Mafia is solidly in control. If there is philosophy in high places there, it is always on a leash.

CONSCIENCE

Split conscience is a form of empathy or partial responsive action in a movement or issue. The Christian minister in National Socialist Germany would feel responsible for the spiritual welfare of his flock, preach his weekly sermon, tend Sunday school, and the like. Yet the fundamental social upheaval resulting in multiple degradation, incarceration and finally gas-choking of a million Jewish and Gypsy children touched not the minister of Christ. He preached with regularity; he blessed Hitler's weapons as requested; he planted Hitler's hooked-cross standard right at the altar. The minister's conscience had split: it covered only one phase of his life. For the great bestialities of street and death camp, he had no eye; for tortured voices of aliens, no ear.

The world is full of people with split conscience. The Communist party leader in Russia as well as in all other countries narrows down the scope of conscience to acts of party discipline and party directives. When the party boss decides to attack a particular fascist, the Communist functionary will join. However, at any given moment the party boss may decide, whatever his opportunistic reasons are, to swing about and only praise the previously defamed dictator. The average Red functionary will follow suit; thus Hitler, Stalin's rabid opponent, became the Communists' friend and military ally.

Such split conscience, reserved for certain limited responsibilities only, is the tragically dominant element in human society. Thus we can observe that the German members of societies for the protection of animals would choke to death Jewish or Gypsy infants with equanimity. Russian scientists leading a life of dedication to knowledge would encourage by signed appeals to American students the assassination of American statesmen and demand the extermination of Jewish émigrés to Israel.

Leftist lawyers who are most sensitive to the refusal of a passport to a professional rabble-rouser in America fail to see the total suppression of freedom of travel in the Leftist countries.

They all live with a split conscience. Nothing matters to those so bereft but their own carefully guarded limits of opportunism. Only in such a world is it possible that highly educated Roman patricians could enjoy a circus of wild beasts devouring captives of another race, or Russia's intellectual leadership supply deadly booby traps and long-distance missiles to reckless guerrillas, or the disciplined churches of Europe put thousands of families of the faith of Jesus to the rack and torch.

I am speaking of the nice people, the educated people, who made no move to free the serfs of Europe or the blacks of the Americas. Where were they, the gentle members of society, those in uniforms, in black cloth, in stylish dress, those on horses and those in carriages—where were they when nine-tenths of the population of Europe, Asia and the Americas lived in squalor and anguish? Where was their conscience? It was split near the edge and that little was dedicated not to man at large, but to their own social equals and interests.

The *crux* will not *salve* this horrid globe of ours; Conscience is the true crux of the matter. Without an all-embracing conscience, undivided and undistracted, the world will remain in miserable shambles with hyenas and vermin on the prowl.

Let the whole conscience speak:

I do not wish to please the clergy. I do not wish to please the saints. I do not wish to please the judges. I do not wish to please the official regiment. I have seen fifty priests and ministers sit around a fettered heretic and rip the living trembling creature's skin off inch by inch. I have seen a group of black-robed administrators of justice condemn men and women on their assembly line of justice to Siberian death camps and Chinese executioners ax heads off on acclamation. I have seen men robbed of their livelihood by the stroke of the pen of subservient superiors. I have seen men butchered in the name of Jesus, Marx, Hitler, Mao, Caesar, the Pope and evil little kings.

I do not wish to please anyone but my conscience.

My conscience does not murder.

My conscience is clear.

My conscience is my guide.

May your conscience replace the dogmas of a torturous world. It has no ax to grind.

CONSCIENTIOUS OBJECTOR

The wish not to bear arms against a real or alleged enemy of the state is as old as man's instinct for self-preservation. The history of conscientious objection to war is rather young. Up to the end of the eighteenth century, all of the "civilized" nations such as England, Russia, France, Prussia, Austria, Spain existed under more or less stringent despotic rule, and a refusal by a laborer or peasant-serf, burgher or clerk to submit to a royal command would be tantamount to suicide. Even at this date, only in the Anglo-Saxon countries are public group objections to military service tolerated and there restricted to certain Christian sects, such as the Quakers and the Jehovah's Witnesses. The military authorities of the West are fully aware that there is nothing in the teaching of the Christian churches prohibiting warfare; indeed the chronicles of warfare read to a considerable extent like chronicles of religious wars. The churches have never hesitated to bless arms, be they the arms of the macabre Louis XIV, the lusty Catherine II or for that matter the maniac Hitler. Nevertheless, a few of the Christian fringe sects set some of the Judaeo-Christian precepts above others: "Love thy enemy" above "I do not come to bring peace but the sword" and honestly sat back in their refusal to fight. This being a truly noble gesture, the question arises, is such sulking ethical?

If such war resistance is intended to stop military attacks on peaceful neighbors or a defenseless people, then surely conscientious objectors have risen to the very spires of morality. Yet we can search in vain among the two hundred fifty millions of Stalin's Russia for one objector to his wanton attack against Finland or among the seventy million Germans for one objector to his rape of Poland. We did, however, have cages full of objectors to our government's military efforts toward stopping the Nazi hordes or containing the communist dictators. Demosthenes, the noble Greek, complained bitterly of those who refused to bear arms against the threatening Macedonian conquerors, putting forth a kind of tepid morality as excuse.

Those who refuse to fight oppression are theologically uninformed if they hang their decision on a gospel quote, are thoroughly indolent if they point to the ubiquity of wars in history and simply frightened if they tremble at the possibility of having their skin cut. All persons ready to go to war—any manner of war, and all wars are horrible—are religiously troubled, personally annoyed and frightened. But morality comes into play not when the reckless gamble with danger but when the thinking person chooses with uneasy heart the road of possible death, mutilation and poverty instead of acquiescence under despotism.

COSMOLOGY

We know not how the world began. What matters is, how will it end?

COURAGE

Courage is not lack of fear but conquest of fear.

CREDO QUIA ABSURDUM

That dictators and religious charlatans demand acceptance of absurd propositions is as old as history. New, perhaps, is the acceptance of the absurd by men of considerable intellectual achievement. The party clique of the Kremlin present their subjects—citizens they are not, since they lack the most primitive premises of freedom to speak, write, travel or vote—with appointed candidates whom they now have the privilege of electing. Yet such childish flim flam is explained with serious demeanor by scholars, scientists, writers, educators in all Soviet lands as "people's democracy." It is, of course, highly opportune to play the game of make-believe with the Red despots as it was in antiquity with the Caesars.

What progress can have been made in political freedom if the Red pundits are punks in civil affairs and unadulterated lackeys of a ruthless power-greedy camarilla? Membership in the almighty Writers Union, a choice job in academy or industry can make the learned graybeards jump like trained monkeys to the Kremlin's command.

CRIMINAL CURIOSITY

Criminal curiosity or the desire to watch cruelty perpetrated on others is prevalent and always was prevalent in times and places of tyrannical unjust administration. In 1724, for instance, two Jewish women were subjected by the Inquisition authorities in Palermo to the auto-da-fé or execution by slow flames. The demand was so great for admission tickets to watch this public act of bestiality that the Catholic Church erected special boxes on high stilts for visitors of the upper classes.

Such criminal curiosity is well known to us from the Caesarean era; indeed Caesar's first public position was chief custodian of the Roman circus. The intense public interest in viewing the guillotine at work at all stages of the French Revolution; the immense crowds assembled in Mao's China in the marketplaces when public decapitations of "opponents" were held; the vicious eagerness with which highly connected Germans sought admission to watch the agonies of Jewish women and children gassed by the Himmler-Eichmann command; they all are indicative of criminal curiosity.

The teachings of hate that emanate from certain political literature or church texts, especially the Gospels interspersed with diabolic anti-Jewish utterances (such as Jews are children of the Devil), create a feeling of delight at the suffering of Jews or other "enemies of the people," remove all human inhibitions, and replace tender attitudes with blatant animosity. The reason for my mentioning the ill fate of the Jews so often is that they have suffered more than any other people the sting of Christian hate for almost two thousand years, and still do!

CRIMINALS

Criminals are not touched in the head as some psychiatrists want to make us believe; they are touched in the pocketbook. What matters the little pickpocket in comparison with the grand thieves and murderers like Hitler, master-marauders Mussolini and Stalin or even the ancients like Caesar and Alexander? The grand criminals were certainly not mentally ill; neither are the little ones. The millions of impoverished people steal to eat; the grand ones steal to revel amid palatial possessions and pompous pretense.

48

The process of equalization begins at both ends: boost the impoverished masses to a livable standard and kick the Führers and Comrade Chairmen off the pedestal.

CROWDS

Those who watch the king's coronation are likely to watch with equal enthusiasm the king's execution.

CRUCIFIXION

The New Testament teaches love to the world and hate of the Jews. This sordid tale of a Roman execution is designed to separate the Jew from the rest of the world and make him the target for hate and suspicion. This has become the core of Christian theology: the hanging of Jesus on the cross at the behest of the Jew. Redemption, resurrection, all the Catholic sacraments are fundamentally based upon this hanging or crucifixion, for which of course there is no evidence at all in history, archeology or literature, except the New Testament, put out in the fourth century by the Bishop of Rome.

Christianity is the one religion of all times based not upon God but on the gallows. Buddhism is dedicated to the life of an ascetic prince; Confucianism to the society of order; Taoism to a universe of ethereal standstill; Islam to overwhelming devotion to One Prophet; Hinduism to the wisdom of the Vedas; Judaism to the Torah of the sons of Israel —and Christianity to the relentless punishment and persecution of those sons of Israel for allegedly having hung one of their own gentle preachers for allegedly pretending to be God's Son. The church has not yet changed its story; the gospels of the pagan king Constantine, going back to the fourth century, are unchanged in their blasphemous and libelous tale of the Jew as killer of God.

What a dedicated people the Christians are! How many more Hebrews will they massacre? Perhaps the only thing that keeps the Christians together is the hanging of Jesus.

49

There seems to be little else wherein they all agree, except the need for punishing the Jews!

CRUELTY

There are societies for the prevention of cruelty to animals, to trees, even to old buildings, yet none for the prevention of cruelty to Jews. I admit a dog is a man's best friend. A horse is, or at least was, a comrade in arms. A cow is holy to the Hindus and a cat was divine to ancient Egyptians. Yet dogs are not masters of medicine; horses have not captured almost half of all Nobel prizes; neither have cats created the Holy Bible, the mother of the three great religions. Perhaps the Jews are in greater need of protection than animals. Did anyone ever hear of six million cats being gassed? Or horses? Or dogs?

Cruelty is not the beast in man; animals do not display such refinement. Animals are uneducated in the science of "a thousand deaths," are uninitiated in the mysteries of political or religious torture chambers. They are ignorant of a pathological precision that enabled despots through the ages to hang a man seven times by reviving him just when he was ready to expire.

Animals are dumb. Man is intricate. Rousseau argued that man was born good, or rather shall we say, indifferent; indifference is, comparatively speaking, a virtue in a world of perennial cruelties. There are numerous types and shades of cruelty, because cruelty is not an attitude; rather, it is a performance. It is cruel to cut a man's nose off, yet Hindu judges did it for centuries as a form of legal retribution. It is cruel to expose wives with families to public rape; still such was a holy ritual in many temples of Eastern antiquity. It is cruel to castrate promising young men; still it was done by loving parents to obtain for their offspring highly desirable positions as choir boys in the West or as court eunuchs in the East.

Acts of cruelty have been committed by sundry despots

in order to create terror in the minds of their neighbors or enemies. El Cid, for instance, even spread false tales of his atrocities in addition to the ones he really committed. Charlemagne decapitated in one day four and a half thousand unarmed Saxons; thenceforth he was accepted as king and master. Attila buried captives up to their necks in dirt and then had his cavalry ride over them. Napoleon bayoneted to death fourteen hundred Turkish soldiers in Palestine who had surrendered to him under the pledge of freedom, first tying them to trees. Caesar cut off the hands of captive Gauls. I do not wish to trouble the reader with further examples; history is full of them. I understand from some chronicles that professional terrorists were in their private lives often tender and considerate. Cruelty with them was a weapon which they employed coldly and calculatingly.

There is another kind of cruelty, that of indifference: Peter of Russia would send company after company into deadly fire in order to overcome a neighbor's position of defense; Stalin or Mao would kill kulaks and other peasants by the million in order to entrench the dictatorial system among thoroughly uprooted and humbled commune dwellers; Sardanapalus had his favored wives and slaves chained to his pyre as he lay dying.

There is the cruelty of the puny mind that wishes to compensate for his or her inferior situation by committing cruelties on those seemingly successful. The poison-pen writer, the denouncer, the arsonist, the tattler, the fraudulent witness, the defamer, the provocateur—they and their likes are to be listed among the cruel.

And then we face the great protagonists of cruelty, the defenders of racial purity, religious orthodoxy, political conformism, the three pillars of hate.

What made the German brewer appointed by Hitler commander of a Jewish concentration camp throw an infant into a cesspool before the eyes of a desperately kneeling mother and kick the woman to death while the child was still crying? What made the Nazi officers threaten Jewish

51

inmates with redhot prongs if they did not beat their comrades to death with clubs? What made the Nazi doctors cut vital organs out of living Jews? What made the Nazi stormtroopers choke to death a million Jewish children by gas or by stuffing them into hermetically sealed trains?

It was hate poured out from German books and orators for centuries that under Hitler reached its culmination. Hate, fomented diligently and cunningly over scores of decades, finally reached the seething point. The Jew was the killer of Christ; the Jew betrayed Germany to the enemy; the Jew had all the money, etc. So effective has been this type of propaganda and so well prepared was the German mind by centuries of subtle anti-Semitism, that at the rise of Hitler to power, the overwhelming majority of the Germans, erudite and educated better than any other nation of that time, were ready to boil Jews alive under hot showers, choke them to death and make soap of their fat—indeed their monstrosities were so great, they defy publication.

German philosophers like Martin Heidegger, German composers like Richard Strauss, German writers like Gerhart Hauptmann vied with each other for honorary positions in the Hitler government. It mattered to these knowledgeable persons little that if the Jews killed Christ, they were also his Apostles (all the early Christians were Jews). If the Jews betrayed Germany to the Allies, the Jews suffered twelve thousand casualties in the First World War, a far greater ratio than any other group within the German Empire. As to the Jews' having all the money: of the seven million Jews living at Hitler's time, west of Russia, the overwhelming majority were tailors, barbers, peddlers, carpenters, teachers and other small-income persons. But hate is a biased observer. And the German people, nurtured in anti-Semitic literature for centuries, became totally obsessed with the devil Jew.

What explains the cruelty of Nazism has direct bearing upon all such racial or religious persecutions: Hate is the mother of cruelty. Foster hate; cruelty will be born in due order. If hate is ripe, cruelty is abundant. All men and all women are prone to cruelty if they are given to hate.

CULTURE HEROES

Cultural achievements are possible in despotic society as well as in democratic environments. It is a fallacy to equate cultural emptiness with tyrannical government even as it is folly to assume culture must bloom in a tolerant and democratic environment. History shows that antiquity's most astonishing creations were produced under ruthless absolutism in pharaonic Egypt. Germany's scientific, musical, philosophical and literary preeminence for a century flowered under the Kaiser's aegis. In Stalin's Soviet Russia, as well as in the Czar's Russia, music of the very best, the ballet, the drama, the novel, technology and science reached phenomenal heights.

The artist and scientist are often—quite, quite often—dominated by their personal career, their personal position in society, and rarely, very rarely indeed, will they exchange the opportunities open to them for a life of revolt and opposition. Leading scientists of Soviet Russia as well as artists of Nazi Germany accepted their "objectionable" leaders, signed public statements for them shot through with vicious propaganda against true liberalism, and refused to notice the widespread persecution of minorities and protesters. It is a melancholy, a triste task to emphasize the obvious fact that with very very few exceptions the artists and theologians, the literati and scientists are deeply engrossed in their own careers and for that very reason will twist and turn so as not to lose their grip on the official rope that leads to personal progress upward.

So much greater should our admiration be for those few, those very few, who ignore opportunism and take up the fight for truth and integrity. Perhaps the time will come when mankind will judge a man by what he does for society, not for himself, and recognize that true achievement lies in helping the community, not one's own professional career.

CZARISM

Under the Czar, the worker fought for the right to strike, to arbitrate, to demonstrate, to appeal to the law, to change his job, to occupy his own separate home, to organize in his own unions. Under the Soviet regime, the worker has none of these. Nor has he even got the Czarist privilege of fighting for them.

DARWINISM

Nature made the rabbit fast so it could escape the tooth of the fox, but how about the poor fox? How is this one supposed to make out? It is not much better than the fundamentalist theorem: God made everything for the good; even evil, such as pestilence and war, God put into the world to punish man or to show off the great good by contrast.

Darwinism is no less anthropocentric than biblical fundamentalism. Darwin looked upon nature, God and man as if all the universe came into existence to produce man. Man appeared to him to be the peak of creation with all the rest forming some sort of ladder of development and significance.

The sad truth is that man, like any other modus, is just one speck amid billions in the universe, lifted on the crest of a mountainous unknown wave for a few fleeting moments, only to sink and disappear like any other grain of sand.

How arrogant sometimes these sand specks act!

DAYDREAMS

Daydreams mirror man's soul. O dreams of youth, harbingers of nobleness, happiness—linger on, linger on! When dreams are gone, this world becomes a dreary place.

DEATH

It is the young who should think of death, not the old. Contemplation of death may sway those full of life; it can affect little those withering away.

Death, like love, should be beheld in silence. Talk in the face of mystery trivializes both the sublime subject and the participant.

DEBATE

No defense is better than a poor one. Don't argue with one who has an ax to grind. He wants the prize, not the truth. Give him silence.

DECALOGUE

The message of the Ten Commandments is compelling but far from being ethically exhaustive. The first five are for the glory of God and parent, which is commendable. The second five concern themselves with people and are woefully inadequate.

Not to kill is a noble request, but if the fighters for freedom had not killed, they would still be carrying leg-irons.

It is ignoble to steal, but then again, the nobleman need not steal while the commoner often must. Theft has often in past centuries been less an indication of the commoner's sinfulness than of the nobleman's greed. It is a poor precept that overlooks the criminal exploiter and brands the victim of the crime instead of the perpetrator. There is not a wisp of admonition against oppression in the Decalogue.

It is a crying offense to bear false witness; but a thousand times over, neighbor has testified against neighbor before the feudal lords. The earls and barons and dukes were the law unto themselves and whoever bore witness against a fellow villein mocked justice by speaking truth in their court. For thousands of Jews, before the great liberation of the western world by the revolts of the eighteenth century and even in our own times where two-thirds of the world live under totalitarianism, the law has been a handmaiden of tyranny. More often a false witness has been able to save his neighbor from condemnation while a misguided truth-seeker has helped to convict the innocent.

The two precepts regarding adultery and desire of the other man's wife, house, servant or animals are commendable, but hardly commandable.

It is possible that in the centuries before Ezra the Scribe, rulers of Judea expunged the other ten instructions:

Do not enslave fellow man.

Do not put yourself above fellow man.

Do not injure the weak.

Do not submit to the Evildoer.

Where there are strong, be on the side of the weak.

Judge not your neighbor by the color of his body.

Do not arrogate to yourself the law that belongs to the people.

Respect the freedom of all and the privilege of none.

Bar none from the road to the top.

Be ever helpful and compassionate.

DETACHMENT

It is commonly held that personal detachment from a cause, any cause, is a sure sign of reason at work, while indeed detachment is only an indication of gross indifference. The Hebrew sage said: "Nothing is easier to bear than the suffering of others."

DICTATORSHIP

The regime by "elected" tyrants may be no less bloody than that of hereditary suppressors. Often in history the men who ripped the chains off an oppressed citizenry used those very chains to rob the liberated of their freedom—from Napoleon to Mussolini, from Stalin to Khrushchev, from Mao to Tiso!

At no time in human history was there a greater number of despotic governments in power than today. From East

Germany to Red China, from Iraq to Algiers and beyond, stretch belts of oppressive governments in which any nonconformist utterance may bring the speaker or writer incarceration or worse. The Marxist despots of today are no less rigorous than their ancient predecessors. They certainly are more sanguine. Indeed, killers on the Hitlerian or Stalinist scale are unknown in ancient times. The slaughter of one million Jewish children by the Nazified Germans and their helpmates (French, Polish and Ukrainian authorities) remains unparalleled in history.

DIET

I suppose that when the good Lord set on this earth animals to be man's food, He had a notion of what the people would like to eat. Carnivorous dinosaur, anyone? Or duckbilled hadrosaurus, looming tons-fat? Giant armadillos, megalosaurus, or stuffed crocodilian—all are difficult to imagine as man's favored dish. I rather think that Adam and Eve dined on grain and berries, with an apple or two for dessert.

DISCOVERERS

For many outstanding figures of invention and discovery, their particular specialty was the only light spot in an otherwise foggy mind. Christopher Columbus, *per exemplum,* once stated that he who possesses gold has also the means of rescuing souls from Purgatory and restoring them to Paradise. *Sancta stupiditas!*

DISLIKE

We do not know why we like some persons, dislike others—this in spite of all our rationalizing.

DOGS

The dogs will bark even if angels sing.

58

EDUCATION

Schools are still run the old Roman way: Learn rhetoric and learn skills; leave the rest to family, church and state. So when a generation ago the first black child was forced into a white school, the white high school girls broke into tears: how bitter to share a classroom with Blacks! The family created the bitterness; the state established separation by law; and the white church remained silent, the silence of indifference. When a generation ago the Christian nations of Europe saw swastika militiamen drag the children of their Jewish neighbors to certain death by fumigation, they shed no tears, wailed not, protested not. They had heard preached for two thousand years as gospel truth that Jews were children of the Devil, who do the Devil's lust. Their families confirmed it again and again in word and sneer and deed. From Poland to France, the Christian states uttered no protest at the barbarous massacre of their Jewish citizens, not even of the infants. Indeed the security officers of those Christian states rounded up the hapless women and children with extraordinary diligence for delivery to the execution trains. These were good Christian states. All cooperated in choking to death millions of women, unarmed civilians and one million children of David marked by Jesus as the salt of the earth, marked by God as the Chosen of His Heritage, but marked by the New Testament the enemy. Hitler prevailed, even in the churches. The cardinals and bishops berated the victims for having crucified "their" Jesus and Pope Pius XII refused to drop his "neutrality." Not one sound, not even a whisper from the Vicar of Christ, descendants of whose own family awaited in the muck of German camps their day of suffocation.

59

And still the schools of Europe after all that dreadful Nazi experience have remained unchanged! Europeans continue to flock by the thousands to Oberammergau, where former Nazi agents put on a show of crucifixion in which all Jews are hook-nosed, vicious and greedy and the non-Jewish Romans wear white togas over their lederhosen. And the churches consider it bad taste to bring up the old charges against Nazism. They want us to forget the massacre of six million Jews, but they can't forget the alleged killing of one Jew. If these Christians of Europe really want to raise generations different from the Hitlerites and Stalinists, they must teach them differently.

They have to teach them not only how to make a living but also how to live; how to live in peace with fellow man. They have to teach them to beware of demagogues who have honey on their lips and poison in their hearts.

And they have to teach them that any priest or preacher who preaches sermons on the Jews being killers of God is a foul-mouthed spreader of malevolence who should be driven not only out of the sanctuary but also out of town. They have to teach the young to be watchful for the hate mongers; only then will they have peace.

Peace does not come by itself. It has to be fostered, cultivated, taught. Teach peace and tolerance, as you have been teaching prejudice and hate. Teach people persistently and daily. It is by far the most important topic in pedagogy. Plant the seeds of tolerance in the young. He who does not plant peace will harvest war.

ENHANCEMENT

The urge for enhancement of either oneself, an institution, or a third party is the most fundamental enemy of truth in communication, especially in countries under a disciplinary police regime where, by writing unwanted text, the writer not only dis-enhances his position but endangers it. Even in the Western World, where a free writer is not threatened by the

60

authorities with incarceration or confinement among the insane with the pain of the accompanying "medical treatment," even in free society where the only danger to the outspoken man is, at worst, loss of a particular job—here too, a man in the academic world will often present a thesis in a manner that tends to enhance his position.

The academic world expects the teacher to publish at regular intervals scientific or literary contributions. Since such papers or books have traditional qualities of form and scope, there appear regularly on the academic horizon examples of literary output for which there are—excepting the urge for, or even need for, personal enhancement—no valid reasons for publication.

It is a sad situation indeed that advancement in academic teaching rank so often depends upon a teacher's ability to communicate with his colleagues through learned journals or books. The best teacher may be a poor writer, and vice versa.

EPISTEMOLOGY

Except in the practical fields and the sciences, thoughts grow in the seedbed of emotions. Traditional prejudicial attitudes and emotions will often make the so-called reasonable person draw horrid conclusions from the same premises on which others walk the path of truth and tolerance.

Hate is the most dominant emotion in social considerations, and the stress of hate bends the rays of thought in distressing, even revolting, directions. Seventy million Germans under this hate impact thought nothing of driving a full million Jewish children into gas chambers and there choking them to death, of organizing the same repulsive execution for five million unarmed civilians, women and men, and throwing the bones and ashes on the dumps of Germany. Yet the very same Germans did not choke the children of their enemy neighbors, nor the enemies themselves. Their prejudicial hate was focused on Jews and the Gypsies, who seemed to them Judaized, if in part only.

Often thoughts take their direction from the emotion of fear and anguish, as in the Communist lands. In the Red "republics," customarily, ninety-nine percent of the population elect the one candidate offered by the rulers, in sheer terror. Subservience is the better part of political thought. Their thoughts on all public issues run closely at the heels of the dictatorial officials. The citizens, or rather inhabitants, have only one concern: Are they close enough in their expressed ideas to the official line, to the desired attitude? Thus entrapped, the Red citizens watch each other for any deviation, no matter how small, because the denunciation of a neighbor's deviation, even an unintentional error, gives the denouncer a "merit" in political conformism. For the reason that thoughts live not in abstract nowhere but in the very humus of emotions such as hate, fear and envy, the Red citizen will praise those presented to him by the rulers as "elected" officials and carry their portraits en masse; he will vehemently denounce those, local or foreign, who displease his rulers; he will not travel abroad for fear of arousing suspicion; he will avoid foreign visitors; he will never, but never, criticize publicly the rulers, the secret police or the military; he will praise an imperialist invasion by his rulers, be it of Tibet or Czechoslovakia, as a brotherly embrace.

In one sentence, thought is a rather unsteady growth from the soil of hate, fear, anguish, terror, ambition, etc. Of course, there are always a few, a very few indeed, who become martyrs of truth and prefer to die erect as did the Jews of Leningrad rather than live on their knees. But martyrs are not the rule, and the heroes of this century by now are all dead or dying. In China and Russia, as in Hitler Germany, jails and camps are only slow methods of execution.

ETHICS

In ancient Chinese script, the symbol for ethics was the figure of a man next to the numeral "2." Only in relation to fellow man can a person act ethically or not. No valid moral

62

judgment of Robinson Crusoe is possible until Friday enters the picture. Robinson Crusoe in his loneness could have been foolishly dissipated or controlled, modest and moderate, or immodestly lusty, imbued with hate and envy or floating on cherubic sentiments, voluptuous dreamer or ascetically resigned—naught of this makes him moral or immoral, just prudent or imprudent. If he had been a Jew, he could have observed all six hundred and thirteen precepts; if he had been a Catholic, he could have become catechism personified and ritual perfected. No matter: ethically he was nonexistent since there was no other person towards whom he could have practiced ethical action.

The master of his own affections, the conqueror of avarice, ambition and lust is still only practicing personal mental hygiene, not ethics. Thus the same master of desire can go out and coldly cut down disagreeable groups or with icy fanaticism annihilate others in his self-righteousness. Innumerable are history's examples of just such events, where fanatics who would not grope for crown, coin, or concubine, in strong silence and inward devotion put virgins to the pyre and men to the stake; and glowering men in the labor leader's tunic, taking nothing for themselves, drive families apart, shunt them into coolie communes, bereft of home, offspring and dignity, and decapitate objectors by the million.

Ethics lies in the deed, not in self-control and not in pretentious social or religious propositions. Most of the religious and prophetic scripts breathe the zephyr of goodness to fellowman, but this breeze of benevolence is blown aside in the life of nations by the overbearing khamsin of ritualism, hate of the disbeliever, and church politics. Many social-reform texts carry messages of fellowship and camaraderie, but soon are they tossed aside by power-fascinated labor czars building up structures of despotism over the working classes. These labor protectors orate about love of humanity and rights of the masses, while they feed the individuals with hate against alleged enemies and rob their followers of every vestige of civic privilege.

63

The church representatives have the love of God yet teach hate of Jews and other disbelievers to tots in the kindergarten. The most dramatic hate story in the world is the tale of the crucifixion of Jesus by a lot of Jews. With its first Sunday school class or first communion, the Christian child learns to fear and detest the Jewish people as the Hindu child learns to fear and hate the flesh-eating Moslems. In this spirit, the Christian infant grows up in love of Jesus, a celestial abstraction, and hate of Jews, a neighborhood reality; as the Hindu gods remain to the child of India a theorem, while the Moslem is found in the market place. Christians in their devotion will calmly kill pagans and heretics, thinking themselves thoroughly dedicated to burning out sin and disbelief.

The root of this and similar evils does not lie in man's bad nature or unwillingness to act morally, but rather in the widespread false teaching of "morality." If men and women were taught throughout the lands, the farms and the cities, that ethics lies in doing good and nothing else, they would destroy the scaffolds, pyres and gas chambers.

No God is worth killing for; neither is any promise of a workers' paradise. And any social or religious system that is predicated upon labor camps, dungeons and the executioner's ax or torch, is neither divine nor humanitarian. Ethics begins and ends right here and not in a coming paradise, heavenly or socialist. The last fifty years have shown as much bestiality in the name of socialist paradise as did earlier centuries in the name of the religious one. What matters in ethics is not the fanciful pretense emanating from above, but the day-by-day action on the ground. And the earth and rivers of our century are full of blood spilled on the altar of various socialisms, as the sky of earlier millennia was full of the smoke of burned martyrs of various faiths.

64

EVOLUTION

We only guess about the origin of man; there is no guesswork about his end. Somewhere here lies a lesson in humility and sobriety.

EXECUTIONERS

As in the days of the Catholic Inquisition, when the "guilty" were made to repent and thank the executioner before the burning for saving them from further torture in hell, the Communist masters of Russia and China compel their victims to debase themselves before the shooting by "confessions" and other kowtow declarations including the inevitable tribute to Marxist justice.

The public axing of political opponents by Mao differs little from the public guillotining by Robespierre. The public was curious enough to watch the proceedings, yet not concerned enough to halt the game of the bloody blade.

How little the world of terror has changed!

EXHIBITIONISTS

This is a generation of show-offs; they even die for effect.

EXISTING

Existing is not the same as living. Look not to lengthen your life but to deepen it. Give it meaning, purpose, not added days of lived-out nothingness. Live your life twice and thrice in dedication to a cause, a vision. So many do not live even once.

EXPERIENCE

The very same experience may serve for one man as impetus to the better, for another as influence for the worse.

FAILINGS

No one sees the failings of others better than the person likewise afflicted. Seneca, Nero's treasurer, the richest man of Rome, published hundreds of tablets on the blessings of poverty; Karl Marx, of Jewish ancestry in both lineages, wrote pernicious little essays against his people, their religion and their character. Mao Tse-tung, in whose domain every house and office must show a wall shrine of his happy countenance and where the official greeting is a heil-Hitler of Comrade Mao's *Quotations,* delivers his most vitriolic remarks against the fostering of personality cults by others.

FAME

Fame is a fickle companion. Often it rides along for only a decade or century. Men were world-famous a generation ago whose names today mean little or nothing; others were hardly recognized in their time, yet their light has grown in spectacular manner. Spinoza, one of the ten very great, died in oblivion but rose a century later above all his contemporaries.

FAR OUT

There is a race of persons totally unrelated—save in one vital respect—to the surrounding real world structure. Some of them, the abstract painters and sculptors, make smudges, circles or dots, wavy lines or spotty blotches, sign the canvas or scratch the stone and that's the total of their artistic life. They care not that no two people will ever identify what they sell with even remote similarity. The abstractionists in art are non-related to anything, except money. There they relate quite well. Their intent is to build up a name, not a creation or a product. Name to them is everything. When they succeed by gimmick or angle in getting a neon nimbus, then a painted soup can or an old tire with their initials on it is money.

Most of the unrelated people are wizards at money-getting. They can squeeze money out of a huge toilet sculpture, a plastic cube or a squeak from an electronic toy. Some of them work in religion, others in psychology. Forever in quest of a gimmick, they discover that "touching" the other sex on a ballroom floor with a hundred "patients" watching is an "experience" with accompanying "release." Religious "workers" with a durable set of tonsils keen about sin and confession and scare the daylights out of the ever-gullible. If someone is scared, he or she will come across with the ducats. How come that after every sermon, there is a collection plate placed in front of the worshipers? How come? These "purifiers" talk as if they had a close familiarity with the good Lord. They can make Him bless you and heal you and even make you lucky at real estate deals and horse bets. You just pay the piper; they'll turn on the hymn and spiel.

The world is full of the people who do things that never touch reality except in your pocket. Some of the "unrelated" engage in stargazing without burdensome telescopes; they just consult sundry yellow-paged pamphlets and write up horoscopes like mad. But so mad they are not; their eyes may gaze afar and beyond, but their fingers are firmly on the till.

Like the fortune-teller or palm reader, the "practitioners" would not have to struggle for petty fees and gratuities if they actually could lift the veil of tomorrow. But those who never die out, the naive gullibles, make it unnecessary for them to work in this real world. It's the age-old-story: the gullible buy a "money-making machine" from a battered old Gypsy without asking themselves the obvious question: why does the old woman have to peddle the machine if she can make her own money?

FEAR

The things you fear most seldom occur.

FEAR OF GOD

Fear of God is a poor substitute for the love of man. They say they fear God, and perhaps they do; thereupon they rush to the business of putting Jews to the torch. The Hindus fear God and kill a million Moslems on the open road. The Moslems feared God and made an end of the Buddhists in India. The Romans feared God and destroyed Jerusalem, because the Jews would not worship Caesar.

We could do without fear of God, without any fear of any God, had we just simple love of man to man.

FICTION

Most novelists have little more than a facile pen and beguiling imagination.

FLAG-WAVERS IN REVERSE

When they talk negatively, be it about nucleonics, militarism, education, civil rights or such, they say "in the United States," although if we have one barrel of garbage in front of the house, others abroad are likely to have a ton. Yet when they talk about achievement, those same commentators say "in the Western World," no longer "in America."

FORGIVENESS

You can not forgive a crime committed, only a crime omitted. If you forgive the evil done, evil will come again, and soon.

FORTUNE-TELLERS

Fortune-tellers, astrologers and suchlike prophets are usually impecunious people; the author of *How to Get Rich Quick* died in the poorhouse. Unless, of course, they "catch on" to be enriched by the fees of the gullible or of cynical news syndicates.

FREE WILL

To see the better—yet to follow the worse. The worse is often a better choice for the thoughtful man. To speak out for the truth is often not opportune; then the hesitant tells himself "silence is golden," while it is only yellow. Courage of conviction is rare indeed; how inviting the hallowed adage which will close your lips!

FREEDOM

Those who are bent on destroying freedom are most vociferous in denouncing its alleged suppressors.

FRIEND

One true friend will make your life richer than a hundred acquaintances.

FÜHRER SYNDROME

The growth of a revolutionary approach to society, seemingly fired mainly by an ambition for a principle or cause, into a personal ambition to dominate the "movement" could be called the führer syndrome. Stalin and Mao, Hitler and Mussolini are classical examples of the humble, selfless party devotee turning into a conniving, dominating party führer. It is those power-mad "leaders" who don a common soldier's tunic under which they hide the dagger of unmitigated terror that enables them to control their handy ruling clique and through them the wide masses. These unimpressive comrades, rodents of society, do their preliminary work underground. Knowing the value of party politics and the political machine, step by step, they rise in votes and influence. They carefully replace regulars with their personal agents until suddenly they stand there in the drill tunic holding the scepter of supreme power in hand.

Hitler in 1933, Stalin in 1927, Mao in 1947—there these führers stand, masters of political intrigue; the innocuous brown rat has grown into a huge eagle, a bear, a dragon! Such is the tragedy of the twentieth century that in half of the Eurasian continent, the rats are lionized, and in those Red countries—appropriately so-called, with their overflow of blood—the portraits which decorate schools, homes and offices are those of führers whom no one elected, although some played the Marxist game of running for office on a one-party, one-candidate ticket. They call that People's Democracy; no one has a choice, but everybody throws a ticket in the box. Since there is no opposition, at least not a live one, it is not surprising that the führers win by a landslide.

FUTURE

Live not in the past, the past is gone; nor in the future, it may never come.

GENERATION GAP

Our society suffers not from a generation gap but rather a degeneration gap.

GENTILES

If the Jews kill a gentile, it's an outrage. If the gentiles kill a million Jews, it's overzealousness. Besides, who can prove the exact number anyhow?

GENTLEMEN

It is not the bestiality of Hitler storm troopers that is so depressing as is the cold-blooded Jew-baiting practiced by some German, French and British gentlemen of that era. The Junkers, the Pétain clique, the Cliveden set—there's the real *canaille!*

GLORY

Some sweat half a century for a decade of glory, yet at the end of the road they, too, are but a heap of dust.

GOD

God is not dead, just sick to His stomach. If God were dead, would we be His only survivors? His heirs? God help us!

God is not a rich man. So many of the Christians have in days of old erected palaces fit for kings wherein to worship the Lord. This was in part due to the concept of God as sanctifier of aristocracy and monarchy. Many of the greatest cathedrals were erected, so to say, as adjuncts of the palace. Some kings, like Philip II of Spain, even had private passages to the altar. God sanctifies the despot and the ruler upholds the church.

I doubt if the Lord prefers His palaces to the houses of the poor people, of whom he made so many. God is not a rich man. He needs neither crown, orb nor scepter. And all His images in gold and glitter on the church walls and ceilings bear not His face at all. God is all Spirit and the Soul has no face.

God's face has been described by many who can barely envision His heels. God is most difficult to come near to, be it by cognition or compassion. Yet some evangelists and others of the profession speak of Him and His many mansions as if they had been born and raised there. They speak with a mouth full of arrogance of God's purpose and will as if they were party to His celestial intent.

I wish these confidants of the Lord would carry their confidence game into more prosaic fields. I hate to see jackasses where angels fear to tread. God is not a member of any religious congregation, yet some dull ministers act as if He were. He is neither a Catholic nor a Protestant nor a Moslem—not even a Jew. Yet He chose the Jews. Some priests and ministers talk as if He were their roommate, as if they knew all His plans and purposes. God likes the silent clerics best, because they don't betray what He never told them.

God has no friends but the true believers. The ancient Greeks called Olympus the lonely rock.

GOD'S NAME

God: what a nebulous word for a lightning-like concept! Men have risen in it like Spinoza to the ultimate heights of intellectual ecstasy—and with the word God on their lips men have sunk to nefarious torture of fellow creatures. The word God is only an emphasis, not a thesis.

Whenever I hear the word God, I become apprehensive. In my travels through history and present-day lands, I have met this Word on sacrificial stones in ancient Greece where a woman's throat was cut into bloody shreds for the alleged divine purpose of bringing peace to a threatened town or to calm turbulent seas. I have met this Word in Renaissance England screeched at dissident believers put to the torch by fervently praying executioners. I have met this Word thundered from German pulpits at devout congregations to convince them that gassing and hanging a million Hebrew children and their unarmed parents and grandparents was fulfillment of a divine sentence on evil anti-Christian paganism. I have met this Word in tragedy as well as comedy, in silly processions of Austrian peasants carrying a painting of a youthful madonna, begging her intercession for climatic improvement by hymn and hosanna. I met it at the toothless mouth of a self-styled holy man, proving his piety by resting on nail-studded boards; I heard it as the vicious shout of an infuriated Hindu putting a Moslem to the knout for butchering a cow. I heard it hurled by a dedicated Janissary piercing the chest of a European and returned by an ardent Crusader slicing the hand off a Mohammedan with knightly grace and religiosity.

Thus, truly, God is a nebulous word, signifying only that the speaker or writer intends emphasis. There is no deed so dastardly that it has not at one time or another, in one place or another, been referred to as "godly." In India a tribe still lurks in the hills which demands of aspirants for membership at least one act of godliness by killing a grown person. Headhunters have often explained their peculiar quest as a godly command.

Alas, how gentle, how trivial, appear those savages in comparison with the great divines of Europe who put whole armies of men and women to a torch, garrot, gas or wild-beast arena in defense of the good word: God. More people have thus been liquidated for a *word* than ever for a deed. The Catholics burned Protestants for not respecting the word; as new successors of Peter, the Protestants in England burned others for respecting it. The Germans gassed the Jews for pronouncing the word Jehovah as they had from time immemorial; the Hindus clubbed to death Moslems for holding on to the word Allah while the Chinese axed anybody who refused to drop their gods for Mao. Perhaps it would be wise to forego the word God altogether, since it may mean a multitude of things and therefore means nothing.

If I hear the words "in the name of God," I become terrified. To me, as a student of history, it sounds like "in the name of Caesar" or "in the name of the Central Committee of the Communist Party" or "in the name of Ferdinand, King of Spain and Defender of the Faith." These sentences invariably preceded the executioner's sword. "In the name of God" is just an arrogant and pretentious way of saying "in the name of whatever I think is important." Because what follows usually has nothing to do with any supernatural being, but rather strictly with local politics, prejudices and sundry other mundane considerations. Preachers in the South argue in the name of God that the Bible is segregationist; of course, in the North where it is safe, the sermons run in the opposite direction. Mullahs in the mosques of Cairo admonish their kneeling flocks that Allah wants a jihad to drive the infidel Jews into the Red Sea, while Buddhist monks of Saigon chant in the name of God for rocks on the heads of the Catholics. Even Chairman Khrushchev swore in the name of God that Communism is a pacifist movement that abhors nothing more than missiles and rockets.

If for no other reason, the word God should be dropped because it lends pathos and dignity to propositions that frequently would tumble under their own flimsiness without the theological prop. Maybe the latter-day Greeks in the Socratic era had found the way to abolish Olympian aristocracy. They merely elevated almost everybody and everything to the status of celestial figure. Serious researchers have listed over two thousand major, minor and minute celestials from gods to sybarites, from half-gods to nymphs. They invested every spring and dale, every tree and lake, even the cemeteries, with one deity or another. And to make sure that no one took this polydeification seriously, they endowed the Olympic characters with an abundance of sin and lustiness, so that even the most naive of Greeks could not wish his family to seek guidance from such adulterous, perverse and selfish divinities.

These gods not only slept promiscuously with each other's wives, sisters and brothers, they fornicated with bulls, swans, horses and goats. Even statues were not safe from their sodomistic yen, nor were members of their own sex. Naturally, when a Greek used the word god, he said it tongue-in-cheek and with a smile. Who could pray to Zeus sneaking home from a sexual romp with the boy Ganymede or a bestial pass at princess Europa?

The Greeks, and with them, the Romans, inflated the word god *ad absurdum*. No wonder the Caesars of the Tiber city placed their own statues in the temples. The imperial monsters would take no back seat to the gods in either voluptuousness or perversion. The word God has outlived its own life of uncertainty and misuse. It is time to place it on the shelf of our tragicomic past, together with the tripod of the Delphic Oracle and the manual for inquisition of witches.

Without this word, God, which has a miraculous capacity of filling void and vacancy even in the emptiest of heads, is it possible that then only those will speak or write on profound matters that have something profound to say? I wish the day would come when this word would be prohibited. They prohibited four-letter words; let it happen to a three-letter one. It should be punishable to use the word God. Perhaps the Jews of old had the right idea by making it unlawful to speak or write the name of God. They referred to Him only as The One, The Creator, The Eternity. You could not as easily abuse those philosophical and cosmological terms for all the thousand evil and shallow purposes to which the word God has been applied.

No one knows the attributes of Creative Nature. The bishop knows no more than the beggar, the savant no more than the servant. The rest is all talk. The attributes of Creative Nature are hidden from the soul of man. The best man can do is follow the road of kindness and generosity pointed out by the great ethical leaders and by his own conscience. There are many laymen and professionals alike who seem to self-glory in evangelism and bandy about the name of God, some-

75

times like a threatening stick and sometimes like a piece of sugar candy. They know no more and no less of the essence of creation than the dullest of their listeners; but they are imbued with cunning audacity which is matched in scope only by the gullibility of their audience.

GOD'S WILL

In Jewish religion, the welfare of man comes ahead of the Law of God. In some Christian seats two thousand years ago the motto was to kill the Jew. The adherents of those denominations felt they were obeying the will of God in avenging an alleged misdeed of some Jews by persecuting their descendants unto the thousandth generation. To those I say, "If God wants you to kill man, turn about; let man live and kill God."

GRACE

Thank not the Lord for placing a full table at your knees; pray rather to Him to become host to the other half of the world which is hungry, homeless and deeply injured. Prayer for your own good and in your own behalf moves neither God nor Devil. Let your prayer for fellow man be a beginning of help for your fellow man.

God is not in need of your grace but half of the world is in need of bread. Send the poor a loaf of bread and the Good Lord will forego your prayer.

GRADING

Grading of students, the very young as well as the adolescent, in public or before their peers, is a constant source of humiliation and hurt to helpless children. Some children are slow-witted or poor in concentration; they can as little help it as those who are nearsighted or hard of hearing. Nature has given out its gifts, physical as well as mental, with uneven hand. Let us help the less endowed, not emphasize their weakness. Even phlegm may be physically conditioned. Let not the teacher ridicule or denigrate the child less favored by nature and background. Public grading implies public degrading. Some educators act as if the child owed the state a high mark! The taxes of the citizenry keep up the school to serve their children, not the other way round.

Publicly marking the students as backward, incompetent, unable, and so on, arouses in youth anger, envy and frustration. How would you like to walk for ten or twenty years of your life publicly marked as "inferior" or "barely passing" or "failure"? Public marking of students helps not their learning capacity, nor does it deepen their intelligence; it only calls forth among children the ugliest traits of competitive envy and makes rifts in human solidarity. In a free society like ours, far better means can be found of pedagogic encouragement than driving children like racehorses or racing greyhounds. You would not like to wear the dunce cap among your peers. Don't put the dunce cap on the children! Grade them not before their peers, that you not degrade them before community and family.

Perhaps it would do you good to study the history of our great men. It might astonish you to find out that most— repeat, most—of the truly great men were mediocre in school, men like Albert Einstein or Winston Churchill, while thousands of class valedictorians turned into selfish windbags and empty arrogants. It is far more important how you learn than what you learn. Treat the children as you want them to treat adults: with dignity, respect and as free members of a free society.

GREAT BOOKS

Many of the so-called great books in history are full of pretense and bombast. There is need for a deep reevaluation of world literature, searching for true merit and not traditional fame and notoriety.

Let's clean house and put the so-called great books to

77

the test. Perhaps the great are not so great and perhaps some of the small are not so small. Homer is boring; and Horace, servile; Aristotle, a slaver; Caesar, an arrogant butcher; Marx, an anti-Semitic muddlehead and Freud, a sick old man living in a lecherous dream world.

Let's take the cranks, crackpots and egomaniacs off the top shelf and put some men there of sensibility and substance

GREAT MEN

Some truly great men became so deeply enmeshed in personal cobwebs that it took centuries to break a clear path to them.

GREATNESS

The gods made greatness strictly one-dimensional. One may look up to a great physicist like Newton; looking closer, one may find him full of religious and other superstitions. Writers like Dostoevski or Gogol, delving deep into man's suffering, may show at closer inspection total lack of understanding of the suffering of proletarians of Jewish ancestry. Profound statesmen have been known to consult astrologers and soothsayers; generals have invoked the good Lord in their bellicose projects; and skillful architects have executed childish plans of conceited politicians.

Seen as men, some of the great are very small, and vice versa. Perhaps there are no great men, only great delusions and great illusions.

Man of antiquity, Greek, Roman or otherwise, had his life filled with gods and half-gods who never ceased to interfere with his existence. That at least is what his heritage and his cunning priests taught him.

Priests had no other occupation but to interpret gods and spirits to man; that was their trade. These men with the all-knowing demeanor were soothsayers, stargazers, interpreters

78

of dreams, runes, bloodspots, liver spots, palms and smoke rings.

Ancient man, confronted and confounded night and day by the cunning diviners, readily succumbed to the assumption that every man's outstanding idea, deed or quality was of Olympic origin. If a child was particularly handsome, Apollo was in there somehow. If the child was astonishingly talented, Zeus himself must have essayed one of his quick-change escapades in the form of a swan or a bull. So many ancients attributed their masculine offspring to Hercules that it became a very popular surname. The highly sophisticated Julian clan simply pushed the diverse celestial statues into the background and put Caesar's image up front to shine upon the worshippers. This glorification of "great" men and women did not diminish with the spread of Christianity, although at first Christian canonization and sanctification stressed different attributes such as nobly suffering pagan arrows, enduring burns from open flames, or being fried alive on a huge pan. There are a thousand saints within the fold of the church, however, to even things up a bit. The organized churches themselves tortured with glowing tongs, rack and torch many more people such as pagans, Jews, Moslems, heretics, and the opponents of friendly kings. Perhaps a little less illusion about "great men and women" would have put a halt to sanctifying the misdeeds of the great.

Dismissing the royal monsters of all eras who are referred to as "great"—no message could be forwarded to Stalin unless addressed to the "Leader of the People" [Gide]—it is indeed a fact that most of the truly valuable achievements in medicine and other useful branches of science were developed by the scholarly or dedicated. Pasteur, Leeuwenhoek, Jenner, Ehrlich, Chain were modest persons who often had to fight the "great names" to put their cause over. Reputations then as now could be established by publicity efforts exaggerating the figure or title of a man rather than any achievement of his.

Hitler, his bestiality notwithstanding, had an army of

"great men" in his pernicious service—scientists, philosophers, literati and composers. The great man can be used by the devil himself as often or more than the man on the street.

It is time to stop draping mere people with the Olympian cloak. Let us evaluate them free of publicity humbug as what they really are, *sine ira et studio*. The brainwashed Chinese Communist who sneers at the vanity of King Louis XIV of France for insisting that his wigged image decorate every room in Versailles, shows a different, quite serious demeanor in discussing "Comrade" Mao's predilection for having his chubby likeness affixed to every available wall of the Chinese People's Republic. Intellect is no protector from opportunism; the brainy supporters of Red China accept this foible as an expression of the Great One's love for his comrades.

In days of yore, you saw men genuflecting and kowtowing to the tradition-imposed lords, the Philips, the Elizabeths, the Henrys, the Charleses and the Louises. You saw proud men, accomplished citizens, cringe before the face of hereditary royal scum. It makes one's heart bitter to read about it. Yet today the genuflecting and kowtowing has not ceased. They stand, the same upright citizens, before the Stalins and the Maos in their massed ranks. Court manners have changed, yet the hearts of the people still shrivel before the "Leader."

GROWTH

Some trees grow slowly; some grow fast. None grows into heaven.

GUILT

It is just barely possible that a band of citizen-jurors called together by high priests would pass a judgment of guilty of presumption of divine powers upon one of their countrymen—all of them suffering under the Roman occupation of the southern part of Syria—and that the Roman procurator would condemn the alleged usurper to the Roman form of execution, crucifixion.

Ten thousand times ten similar "offenders"—some innocent, some merely obstreperous protesters—were put to death under Roman rule, but only a pathological fanatic would then shriek, "Let's kill all of the rebels, kith and kin, not only all his family but all his people forever and ever! Let the blood of Jesus come upon all the Jews. The Jews killed Jesus Christ; let all Christians fall upon all the Jews from now until kingdom come!"

GYPSIES

Gypsies are by some considered latter-day Jews. Their origin is only guessed at. Some claim they hail from the northern part of India, others from Egypt. If not brothers under the skin, the Gypsies are certainly the Jews' brothers under the lash. There are historians who maintain that some Gypsies appearing in Europe in the Middle Ages are descendants of Eastern Jews who, under the onslaught of Christian charges of well poisoning, plague carrying and blood drinking, had fled into the forests of the Balkans, where they mingled with Christian villagers.

Gypsies were treated by manorial lords of eastern Europe as vagrants without rights or privileges. Like the Jews, many of them were skilled craftsmen, tinkers and musicians. Like the Jews, they were not permitted to settle but given only temporary stay. And like the Jews, in the final (?) great attack of anti-Semitism they were gassed and burned to ashes by Christian nations of Europe. The Germans considered them *Untermenschen* and the French, Poles and Russians could not have cared less. Only the caverns of central Europe can tell the whole story.

HAGIOLATRY

Every so often the Vatican feels compelled to reduce the number of acceptable saints. It appears that the historicity in some cases is doubtful. Not long past, however, Pope Paul VI proclaimed four new saints who were burned at the stake 600 years ago. They were all Franciscan friars who attempted to convert the Caliph of Jerusalem to Christianity—this, right after the Crusades, during which there was open season on Moslems!

If the Vatican is serious about seeking saints who were martyred in defense of their faith, the Jewish people can supply the Holy Father with a list of almost ten million of Christ's kinsmen who refused to desert their religion (which was also that of Lord Jesus) and thus were put to death by Christian disbelievers over the last thousand years from Saint Vincent Ferrer to Bogdan Chmielnicki and from Torquemada to Adolf Hitler. And these names are all historic; extensive examination of the martyred is hardly necessary.

HALF-TRUTHS

Truth as a whole is hard to take. It is much easier to swallow half-truths. Novelists, dramatists, poets and performers more often enjoy acclaim than the truth-seekers.

HAPPINESS

A man who seeks only his own happiness will find that solitaire is in the long run quite a boring game.

HEAVEN

If I were God, I'd keep away from people. They think heaven is a place where you receive reward for your good deeds and forgiveness for the bad ones. No wonder they all like religion; it's a good deal either way.

HELL

The very idea that God Jehovah, the great embodiment of love, sets monstrous angels of torture upon the souls of the poor deceased, all of them martyrs sinful by mere birth, is repulsive to all Hebrew theology. Whatever heaven there be, God is its all-loving father, not a sinister flame-thrower or breaker of dead bones, directly or by devilish proxy. Dantesque balladizing of torture flames upon lips or breasts and lances through the anus is only sick imagination, not the will of the Lord. The Lord is love and serenity, compassion and devotion, not a pin in the groin.

The painters and poets of purgatory, hell, and inferno bespeak their dark souls and bitter anguish; the face of Elohim, the Father Eternal, is shrouded from them. The face they paint is not of Adonai, Echod, the One, the Lord. Their Devil is not a servant of the Merciful one; it is their own fearsome image.

This Christian image of most revolting torture was actually accepted by all Christian denominations at one time or another. Some militant Christians decided to jump the gun on the torturous perversion promised in the saintly hereafter and put it into practice right here and now. Why wait for hell? Let's have hell on earth! The whole bestial inquisition practice is only a leaf taken in advance from holy scriptures of Christendom. Burning alive of fettered women and children, often in the presence of the parents, indeed the whole ugly scheme of Catholic reprisal on "offenders" or "heretics" was a preview of the great inferno threatening all believers.

Naturally, this threat of the monstrous hereafter gave the

clergy an inordinate power over the people. The Church lorded it over the genuflecting neck-benders, since the clergy held the ladder to paradise; a single misstep on a single rung gave them the privilege of sending the subservients of the church straight down to the abyss of hot coals and bloody prongs. Thousands of paintings, drawings, sculptures, poems, hymns, essays, sermons and open threats were used and abused by vile clergymen to scare the gullible of Europe, high and low, into slobbering subservience.

Hell on earth is no fantasy; but hell is blasphemy. It gives God a bad name.

HERESY

Heresy becomes an offense when it endeavors to verbalize its position. All people are heretics, certainly in theology, since no two persons could possibly ever agree on all points and pointlets of revealed religion. Heretics were marked by official clerical authorities at times and places when the officials encountered resistance to an issue they tried to put across.

In modern times politics has replaced theology; the heretic today in despotic governments is the "religious" heretic of yesterday. Despotism rules by endowing its master with absolute dignity and sanctity. Opposition to Hitlerism in Germany or Stalinism in Russia or Maoism in China has been branded heresy with the same arbitrary authority assumed on behalf of Christian theology. Inquisitions in all of them were very brief and defense irrelevant, as the sole purpose of accusation was elimination of opposition by "authorized" violence by torch, ax or bullet. The Catholic Queen Mary burned Protestant bishops. Her Protestant sister Elizabeth executed Catholics and the monstrous trio, Hitler, Stalin and Mao, axed all their heretics. The Christ-adorers, Protestant or Catholic, managed to find heresy in other Christians; the Marxist trio unraveled heresy in other Marxists. Church literature as well as Marxist literature contains a myriad of contradictions.

Heresy occurs when the dominant authorities are eager to score a point. On such points a million humans have been nailed—and this is not a metaphor.

There is no heresy in civilized society, only assassination of the innocent who refuse to kowtow to imposed interpreters of faith and politics. Luther suggested cutting out the tongues of the Jews if they did not accept Jesus, and the Vatican harbored similar feelings about Luther's heresy. Today it is Mao and Brezhnev whose pronouncements echo that malevolence; yesterday it was Hitler and Stalin. Heresy is made by despots, not by heretics. They are only the unfortunate victims of a cruel society.

HERO

It is the cause that makes the hero, not his courage or his suffering.

HERITAGE

Tradition is not always a reliable guideline to history. Some nations express pride in their heritage of Viking or Norman origin. Many of the Nordics in older centuries were hardly discoverers but rather conquerors, brutal invaders, arsonists and rapists, killers and burglars. Let's not glorify burglary and rapine because we were told fancy tales of conquests and victories. The greatest killers of them all were the Romans of antiquity, who left Gaul, the isles of England, Greece, Egypt, Carthage, Jerusalem and the rest in shambles, men beheaded and crippled, women ravaged, cities in flames, children hiding in forests.

The Romans were the Nazis of antiquity. Why glorify their arenas for gladiators and other beasts of prey? They, the Romans, often massacred a thousand captives in a hundred ways, from crucifixion to burning on flaming poles or spits. Roman heritage is one of indescribable bestiality. Why glorify it? Condemn vicious heritage; do not ennoble it by stress on military victories of Roman militia and mercenaries! Give praise to the sages of old, the fine prophets and the teachers, not the bloody savages of the Roman Empire. The Caesars from Julius to Nero belong in criminal encyclopedias, not in schoolbooks. Where are the great academies of Athens, Jerusalem, Alexandria, Carthage, Syracuse? They were all reduced to rubble, the towns sacked, all art and literature thrown to the flames! All this at the bloody hands of triumphant Roman dictators. Roman tradition is the devil's heritage.

HOLY WRIT

There is a lot of holiness in the New Testament, ancient and latter-day Hebraic wisdom. Yet there are places where some of the biographers give vent to amazing outbursts like calling the Jews sons of the Devil, that "do the Devil's work" (John VIII. 44). Jesus, the gentle Jew, never, never spoke such slander about his own people! Never, for sure!

Indeed, what can be holy about a Greek version of a lost Hebrew text? We have the Gospels only in Greek and Jesus spoke only in Hebrew. We must therefore read the New Testament, be it in English, German or French, as a twice-translated work of biographical character written by simple men who never knew the subject of the holy book or its profound object.

HOUNDS OF HEAVEN

After the conquest of Judea by the Babylonians (586 B.C.) many Jews fled to faraway India where they were well received by the Hindus, given the hospitality of the land. There they practiced their faith and customs for two thousand years. However, in the fifteenth century Portuguese conquerors arrived and destroyed the Jewish community in Cranganore. Many Jewish settlers were put to the sword by the Christian navigators as "the crucifiers of the Lord." Some few escaped to Cochin, where they still live among the gentle "pagans," as the Portuguese styled the followers of a religion two thousand years older than their own.

86

ICONOCLASM

In the fourth century of the Christian era, Constantine made the bishops of Christ masters of the religious life of the whole Roman Empire. Province by province, town by town, the temples, shrines and monuments serving pagan beliefs were destroyed. Some few vestiges of the non-Christian religion were saved by quick surrender to Christian churchmen. The rest were demolished. The major part of so-called pagan religious objects were either crushed or broken. Many of the Roman shepherds, farmers, merchants, artisans, equestrians and patricians buried their god-statues in shallow graves or threw them into the nearest bay to escape punishment by the church authorities. Neither the winds nor the rains were the destroyers of the pagan temples and monuments—the hammers of frightened neo-Christians did the job.

Only Judaism was *religio licita* in Rome of the fourth century of our era. The Jews had nothing to destroy as their faith did not permit them to have graven images of divinities. The Romans called the Jews godless since they had not a single picture of God. While all the many religions of pagan Rome disintegrated under Christian pressure, Judaism lived on, worshiping a God with no face and observing precepts without blood and sacrifice.

I have no strong feelings on the iconoduly that moves believers to cover themselves with amulets, crucifixes, holy bracelets, rosaries and medals of the devotional type. It has often met opposition among the more sophisticated worshipers. Historically, the early Christian did not favor idolatrous images, mainly because of the strong Hebraic influence still prevalent. In time, however, the Roman and Greek polytheistic romanticism with its veneration of statues, symbols and allegories revived and even the hesitant Eastern churches succumbed to iconoduly.

I do, however, have strongly iconoclastic thoughts about another kind of iconism, the secular one blanketing with its venomous miasmas this our poor globe. I mean the glorification and beatification of brazen despots, in statues and pictures, in books and songs, in street names and edifices. It revolts me deeply to find on my travels enemies of republican government like Augustus enthroned as a sculptured god; or the mercenary Campeador El Cid, who massacred the citizens of Valencia, enthroned on a horse; or Queen Elizabeth I, the virgin of London with her coterie of lovers, who played the Fagin for a score of pirates and initiated England's grand schemes of colonial oppression, slave-trading and vassalization of weaker nations, painted as patroness of art and culture.

What lessons can the young learn from history if the most tyrannical, most vitriolic and perfidious despots are daily honored by an iconolatrous and forgetful people? Some of these cynical usurpers practiced their sardonic wit on the naiveté of the commoners: Alexander named a city after his horse Bucephalus; Caligula went him one better by appointing his horse Incitatus a Senator. I am waiting for the day of iconoclasm when the devil's lofty horsemen will be pulled into the gutter, the fratricidal kings and the crimson-fingered queens from Inquisition's Isabella to the lecherous Catherine have their portraits transferred to the cellars of crime museums and our edifices, streets, and forests are renamed after the men who fought for freedom and justice instead of after the slavers and their henchmen.

It is time to cleanse our books and songs, our homes and schools, our streets and churches, even our cemeteries of the symbols glorifying savage princes of the past and to relegate their horrid images to the somber pages of criminal history.

If these offensive statues and paintings of history's so-called great have to remain in public places and public museums, let's at least identify them properly, not by the allegedly great deeds of conquest or plunder but by the real character and real actions of the man in stone or the woman in paint. Let's inscribe Peter the Great's portrait with the fact that he reduced the peasantry of Russia to abject slavery under which they were traded like common property for hounds, cows or horses; that under Catherine the Great the working classes were reduced to similar serfdom so the empress could get her warships from the shipbuilders as a virtual gift.

It is time either to eradicate all traces of these insufferable despots of Europe or at least to let the wide masses know that their school history books are shameful fabrications by subservient elite: that Caesar was an egotistical butcher of tens of thousands of women and children in Gaul; that Napoleon Bonaparte was no less a bloodletting conqueror than his antecedent Louis XIV the Sun King. Napoleon fell upon Europe like Louis XIV and his devotion to freedom lasted only long enough to let him seize power from the people for his crowning self-glorification. Let the wide masses know that a thousand church-protected hereditary aristocracies obtained and held the power in Europe for two millennia, reducing the peasantry to dust-eating serfdom and the workers to hapless handymen, woefully poor, filthy and diseased.

Let's make an end to the farce of iconizing Europe's ignobility and label the tyrants at last for all the world to see as they really were and are.

IDEAS

If man's mind were a reliable thinking machine, sound, correct ideas would have a reasonable chance of coming out on top. As it is, with the human brain mixed up in prejudices, muddled from earliest training by unreliable tutors, parental ambitions and dominant slogans, the chances for average man to come out with logical ideas are rather slim.

IGNORANCE

Ignorance may not be bliss, but knowledge certainly is not either—at least for others. The great despots of the world were and are frequently most knowledgeable men. Mao is a doctor of philosophy; Mussolini was an erudite teacher; Stalin was a well-read seminarian; Hitler an astute student of history and an artist; Rosenberg an academically trained historian and Goebbels a playwright. Pope Pius XII established the theology of indifference, and all the great denominational leaders of Christianity found the Vatican approach highly acceptable. See not the choking children, hear not the outcries of raped women and gasping civilians and say not a word of Germany's atrocities. Indeed, this century has proven that bestiality can enter as easily on the arm of learning as with ignorance.

INCENSE

Light no candles and burn no spices for the glory of God. They carried signs "for the glory of Christ" when they burned Jews. After two thousand years, the Jew abhors the smell of incense.

INEFFICIENCY

Mankind still runs on less than ten percent of its mind cylinders. The overwhelming majority never even acquire the educational tools to participate in cultural activities. They merely serve and die.

INTELLIGENTSIA

It is amazing how many most reputable scientists, scholars and literati have accepted as blessings horrible misdeeds perpetrated by men in power. For instance, the eminent philosopher Martin Heidegger extolled Hitler as the godlike spiritual leader of European civilization; Jean-Paul Sartre whitewashed all, but all, of Stalin's blackest deeds; Saint Augustine demanded enslavement of all Jews because their ancestors rejected Jesus; Thomas Aquinas concurred. The renowned composer Richard Strauss and the dramatist Gerhart Hauptmann considered it a privilege to serve in Hitler's Chambers of Culture; the Italian philosopher Giovanni Gentile based his political theories on "Mussolini, giant among men."

Scientists, artists, writers have grovelled before the dictators of this century. China's educators to a man adopted Mao's *Quotations* as the sole and supreme principle of all pedagogy; indeed it was and still is impossible to attend any cultural gathering in China without hearing the *Quotations* flaunted by speaker as well as audience. Where is the integrity and self-respect of the intellectuals if so many kowtow to so few?

What good is a brilliant mind if it cares little or less who will prevail, Lucifer or Gabriel? Indifference is perhaps the most deplorable failing of man. All about us we see callous genius and masters of technology in the well-rewarded service of despots, helping to confuse the average man with devious propaganda, painting the devil white and the angel black.

ISRAEL

Israel had to discover an old truism: the Christian world has a cold spot in its heart for the Jew.

JEWISH BLOOD

There is no Jewish blood on the altar of any religion except the Christian. The Roman, the Greek, the Carthaginian, the Zoroastrian, the Hindu, the Shinto, the Buddhist, the Confucian, the Chaldean, the Moslem—all had contact or controversy with the Hebrews, yet none but the followers of Christianity rounded up the sons of Israel to burn them, children and all, alive and whimpering. This is the singular attribute of the Christians.

JEWS

God chose the Jews from among all the nations. Hebrew is the only language He used in talking to man. He chose His Son from the people of Israel. God loved the Jews. If you hate the Jews, you do not love the Lord.

The Jews have by far the greatest percentage of scientists, scholars, educators, artists, professionals and skilled manufacturers. The world cannot forgive them for that.

JUDAEO-CHRISTIAN

Judaeo-Christian is one of those ludicrous adjectives created by one who does not understand that Judaism is certainly the antithesis of Christianity, according to basic documents of the New Testament. The word Jew is mentioned in those Scriptures as a vile opprobrium, to wit: The Jew is a Son of the Devil; the Jew is betrayer of his Savior; the Jew is a malevolent disbeliever in Christ; a man of Judea, named Judas, gives the kiss of death; the Jew persecutes Christ, who asks of him pitifully, "Why dost thou hurt me?"

Jesus would not enter Judea in fear of the Jews. The Jews have Jesus apprehended, thorn-crowned and scourged; the Jews press manifold charges against Jesus; the Jews have Jesus crucified and ask Pilate to break the bones of the dying Jesus.

Indeed, of the hundred-odd references to the Jews in the gospels, all are viciously anti-Semitic in effect and intent. So what does "Judaeo-Christian" mean except a slyly concocted expression for a nonexisting union of opposites? Until all those vile anti-Jewish interpolations have been eliminated, the New Testament will remain to all Jews a book of sad contention, a sanguine document of abuse, discrimination and persecution. The Jew is not interested in Christian theology. What does it matter to the Jews if half of Christianity does not recognize the sacrosanct status of the pontiff or the power of other patriarchs in the various Christian hierarchies? They all, no matter on what theological 'isms' they disagree, accepted the Jew-baiting sentences in the New Testament as Holy Scripture. No matter what, *Der Jude wird verbrannt!*

Luther fought the pope tooth and nail, yet to him the burning of nine thousand Jews in Spain at the hands of Catholic inquisitors was no more than an inspiration to demand that all Hebrew books be burned, as were the houses of all the Jews, that every Jew be confronted with the New Testament and if the Jew refused to accept Christ, that he have his tongue cut out. While there are many modern and some older essays pleading for a bit of charity toward the Jew, as far as Christian theology is concerned, there is not a single effort among its representatives to excise the anti-Semitism from their Bible. They probably feel that Jew-hate makes the Gospels more dramatic and gives the "believers" something concrete to hang onto. While the Christians in high places, especially the high clergy and their protectors, have shown little effect of Christ's sermons on love of neighbor, as far as the Jews are concerned they were all—popes, bishops, priests, deacons and ministers—relentlessly engaged in hunting down the Hebrews with fire, rack and sword. In fact, there was only one Bishop of Rome, the blessed John XXIII, who spoke of Jews as people. As a minor aside, Bishop Luigi Carli, a mean anti-Semite of the Mussolini era, was appointed by Pope Paul VI as representative of the Curia on the "Jewish Question" and he publicly, repeatedly, and in published writings denounced the Jews, all the Jews, from infant to the dying as having an "accursed faith," an abomination to God.

So what exactly does Judaeo-Christian culture mean? A few of the Jewish writers of our time (including myself) have made attempts to persuade Christian theologians to support a campaign to excise from the New Testament those hundred-odd anti-Semitic references. The task is technically easy since all that has to be done is to substitute for "Jews" such words as 'crowds', 'people', 'persons,' and the like. The sentence, "The Jews are the Sons of the Devil and do the Devil's work," should of course be omitted entirely. It is annoying to note that the overwhelming majority of even liberal Christian theologians suddenly turn fundamentalist and will hear nothing about tampering with the word of God or "changing God's Holy Scriptures."

Those Jew-baiting remarks by the scribes of Rome in the early centuries are obvious interpolations. I wonder if these men of the black or purple cloth really accept without doubt the Gospel exclamation by Jesus, son of Joseph, son of David, addressed to his family and friends: "You Jews are the Sons of the Devil!" Yet they want the anti-Semitism in their Bible, for the same reason that they are in despair over the Jews now holding Jerusalem. Into their scheme of liturgy it fits that God took Jerusalem away from the Jews through His taskman, the Roman general Titus, and had the general expel the Jews from all of Israel and Judea, and thus dispersed the Jews all over the world as punishment for the crucifixion of His Son. It disturbs the Christian theologians all over the world that the Jews by holding Jerusalem discredit the accuracy of things that were and things that are

94

By holding Jerusalem, the Jews (perhaps deliberately!) make Titus appear as nothing but a typical Caesarian military marauder without the slightest symbolic understanding of God's purpose in Palestine. The Jews also discredit the punitive dispersal of the Jews since already one fourth of their people have returned to their homeland, a ratio no lower than in Titus' time. Yet, the Christian theologians urge with great devotion that the Jews be dispersed and driven out of Jerusalem to prove their hundred anti-Semitic Bible points. If this is Holy Scripture to the Christian clergymen, it is a monstrous litany to the Jewish nation that does not wish its offspring depicted as creatures of hell.

The Christian clergymen teach their youth from the age of six to sixteen that the Jews are all I mentioned before, defilers of houses of worship, torturers, traitors, bone-breakers. How do they then expect those Christian children to grow into normal peace-loving people who love and respect their neighbors, especially the Jewish ones? The trauma of bloody Jews baiting Christ impresses itself deeply into every Christian child and even in later years is seldom entirely overcome. One remark by a single influential person, be it Hitler or Stalin or de Gaulle, and the slumbering snake of Jew-hate crawls out of the pit of the subconscious. The Jewish nation will never live unmolested until the hate has been removed from the Christian Bible.

JUDGING

Judging a man without recourse and reference to his past record is like trying to heal a patient without knowledge of his medical history.

JUS PRIMAE NOCTIS

Privilege of the first night with every desired bride of villein or serf in the manorial territory was widely practiced by the lords of feudal Europe. The amazing element in this

95

wanton abuse of lordly prerogative is not so much its own debasement as the snide assistance rendered the lecherous baronial masters by their clergy, Catholic and Protestant alike. The Christian clergy of feudal Europe put the divine stamp of approval on this abhorrent perversion of the solemn by the gospel citation to the raped populace: "Render therefore unto Caesar the things which are Caesar's." It was not the church but the American and French revolutions which made an abrupt end to the sodomic outrages of a now terrified "nobility." There must be a better word to characterize these palace bastards than "noble."

Two hundred years later, however, *jus primae noctis* came back with the German Nazi movement and went into its second odious phase wherever the German army dominated. Jewish girls from the age of fourteen on were apprehended by the German military in Warsaw, Lvov, Krakow, Budapest, Paris—wherever they conquered—and turned over to SS officers and Einsatz-Truppen for "treatment." These Jewish brides and children, in front of other officers of the German forces, were put through a most sordid process of defloration and then assigned to bordellos in German barracks and concentration camps. The city of New York, the cities of Israel, the cities of London, Paris and Buenos Aires have hundreds of now older Jewish women who were "lucky" enough to survive the blood and horror of rape, the unspeakable years in military bordellos. These women of Israel still carry on their wrists the bordello numbers indelibly engraved.

Rape by soldiery is common enough in history but here the German political authorities planned and organized the deflowering of Jewish childhood and young womanhood with the whole Christian world watching in total, but total, indifference. The Catholic and Protestant bishops not only of Germany but of all Christian Europe from Spain to the Ukraine, from Italy to Sweden, made not a single sign of protest. This ignoring of the public rape of femininity in the heart of Europe must remove from the mind of any thinking

96

person the very last doubt that Christianity is little but a perfunctory procedure of allegiance to an alleged faith that sees nothing, hears nothing and certainly does nothing.

For us Jews this silence of the church speaks louder than words or outcries can. The Pope did not hear or see; the cardinals were talking of holy things. The bishops were concerned with German victory; the priests and ministers were taking confessions from erring servant girls or giving sermons before the altar decorated by Nazi flags or touching scenes from the Gospels. While the daughters of Jacob, of David and Jeshu, were ravaged by Christian Europe!

JUSTICE

Some of the great judicial minds do not see the tree of justice for the forest of legalism. Remember, the law is only a string of words, but justice is the will of Wisdom.

KARMA

The belief in transmigration of souls may lead to acceptance of *karma* or the judgment of man in a former existence of his soul. Unfortunately among the Hindus, where the mainstream of metempsychosis runs, the repulsive caste system is popularly justified by *karma*. These God-ordained Untouchables and low castes of India are as solidly emplaced in the gutter of society by the *karma* superstition as the God-anointed rulers of the earlier Western World on their sumptuous thrones. What spiritual beauty is there in metamorphosis of man's soul as footstool of social oppressiveness?

LAW

The law is not always the servant of Justice.

Often it is the servant of evil masters, like the feudal law, the Nuremberg laws, or the laws perpetrated in the Stalin or Mao era.

Moreover, the law may on occasion become so intricate a maze that it is impossible to get at the criminal, thus nullifying its original purpose.

LEFTISM

It is ironic that the Lefts want all the rights.

LIBEL

You cannot find a single historian in the Catholic Church who will not admit that all, but all, the trials of Jews on the charges of drinking Christian blood at Passover time, of well poisoning, of plague importing, of Host desecration, of urinating into holy water or holy wine, were false, malicious and torture-confessed. Yet, unto this very day, while occasional admissions of these grave injustices are whispered, the Vatican has not the Christian courage to fall on its knees and cry out, *"Nostra culpa, nostra culpa!"* I do not know if confession of guilt expiates a sin, but arrogance certainly does not. On your knees, Rome!

LIES

Truth does not persuade by itself. It is not enough to master the truth. Can you interpret it to others? One faces often in life those who are totally bereft of scruples in logic as well as ethics and are endowed with considerable skills in persuasion. Stalin was fully aware that his comrades in arms were sincere and dedicated revolutionaries, yet in order to gain absolute power over the party and government machinery, he was successful in convincing the Russian people of the opposite and even drove his nation to such a frenzy of hate against the "traitors" that they massacred the most illustrious Soviet Marxists with unparalleled brutality.

Truth is a poor adversary of the Great Lie on the tongue of the skillful. For that very reason, this our beaten globe is still in the hands of the glib, not the true. Millions of innocent little people perish every decade, victims of hate-mongering perfidy promulgated by ruthless demagogues, and often even the sincerely liberal hearken to the false tunes of propaganda; the still voice of truth and profundity dies unheard in the wind. The Lie travels decked out with the colorful bunting of wild promises, artful slogans, catchy denunciations supported by shrewdly fostered personality cults, while the Truth is offered by the philosophically minded in her unadorned and uncorrupted verity. Perhaps this is the destined role Truth must play out in all times, gone and to come, to be protagonist of the Good in the great turmoil of man's existence.

Truth is a lonely traveler.

LIFE AFTER DEATH

It was the custom among the ancient Hebrews to bend the thumb of the deceased so that the folded hand would read like the word *Shaddai,* the Destroyer. This was one of the many circumscribed ways of referring to the Almighty. Death is the great destroyer and thus the great reminder: *Vanitas, vanitatum vanitas!* Even the most sophisticated, even the brazen and reckless, the shameless and the cruel, on their deathbed the awesome nearness of Shaddai touches them and often for the first time in their hasty lives they feel the presence of something overwhelming that makes them realize, too late of course, the emptiness, the nothingness of their unanchored being. The dread of nothingness is upon them.

The ancient Egyptians held that the deceased's heart was weighed upon his entering the Land of the Dead. Similar references are found among the Semitic tribes. One might presume that from those burial trials came the legendary "judgment day" and latter-day Christian mythologies of "sentences" to heaven, hell and purgatory. The Moslems, close to the Semitic theologies as well as superstitions, show traces of the "final judgment." The philosopher Kant found it necessary to postulate such final judgment and immortality. They prevail, because otherwise, viewing the rampant and unpunished injustices in this world, we would have to despair of a wise Providence. Metaphysically, Kant's three postulates of God, Freedom to Choose, Immortality and Judgment, read well, but in reality the number of those who accept a post-funeral existence of the corpse and/or his spirit has dwindled with the speed of light.

The certainly noble concept of a parliamentary justice post mortem has little if any influence on the three billion men and women swarming on this moist rock and can be almost entirely disregarded as an ethical factor. Man must fashion his conduct not in fear or expectation of a hazy mythological *dies irae,* but in respect for fair judgment by his contemporaries and, foremost, in obedience to the soft but clear voice of his conscience. Man's conscience is knowledgeable; man's egocentric nature, however, may often prefer a tempting delusion to the plain truth.

Men don't act evil because they know no better, rather because the worse suits them well. The master of choice rides not in the mind but on the emotional waves of self-interest.

LINGUISTS

Linguists share with grammarians a tendency toward exquisite dullness in selecting exemplars for reading. The Latin teachers have forever clung to the tiresome prose of

Gaius Julius Caesar, an ambitious master of Rome's arena amusements and latter-day bewitcher of Legionaries, usurper of what was thence to be a Roman throne soiled by Caligula, Nero, and such, until swept aside by the mighty migration from the East. Using Caesar's autobiographical notes as reading practice for Latin is like making Hitler's *Mein Kampf* a German reader. A pupil even while studying a foreign language must be made aware of the threats to democracy by tyrannical adventurers. Acceptance of literary calumny as a great example of linguistic art tends to legitimatize the political felon in the eyes of the young. The self-aggrandizement and clever rationalizations of the palace cliques, in no matter what era, belong in our books of criminology and not in our cultural histories, regardless of their being written by the scepter-wielder himself or his scribbling ghost.

LITERACY

Literacy can be used by the oppressor as well as the reformer. America gave the nation overwhelming literacy and thus structured democracy. Russia has used the same widespread literacy to destroy democracy.

LITERATURE

Literature, after clinging for millennia to morality, has of late become enamored of immorality. There always was a hideaway segment of literary outpouring commonly referred to as pornography; one particular century, the eighteenth, in one particular country, France, gave it ample berth. The twentieth century in the Western world has somehow embraced the era of the Marquis de Sade and become so intertwined with it as to appear like the proverbial four-legged monster. Literati, some awkwardly, some shamefully, and some brazenly, load their novels, stories and plays with four-letter words, perverse sexual figurations and such minute descriptions of multifarious genital activities that one suspects they consider their readers sorely in need of either information or titillation.

Of course, thus develops an unavoidable situation: writers of pulp and toilet pornography rise to the top like scum. Looking these days into a bookstore window, one wonders which preponderates— the literati gone pornographic or the pornographers gone literary? All this overspilling from seedy sexographers into the written word is not as harmful as a few claim; however, it has drawn over living literature a fog of unwholesome concentration on genital functions and, be-clouding the older great vistas of novel and drama, has degenerated into awful boredom. Sex of course is part of living, but they are making a living part of sex.

LIVING

Of life we are certain only of the beginning; the end is totally unknown—yet so many talk so much about that phase of being.

LOGIC

Most of us can reason pretty well; the issue is not lack of intelligence but lack of integrity. The leaders of Hitler's Germany were not illogical but rather ignoble. Even some of their "unscientific" ideas such as racism were not based on lack of understanding but rather on deliberate confounding of the minds of the people. Marx's and Stalin's statements that the Jews were all usurers or exploiters are not indications of the ignorance of these two demagogues but rather evidence of their dishonest way of "argumentation." Despotic "leaders" are not suffering from disruptions in their logical cohesion, but rather from lack of conscience and political integrity.

Somehow, by the use of controlled schooling, controlled press, radio and other means of communication, the despots manage to confound average men and women and by deliberate incessant propaganda to bend the people's minds into accepting and even praising their crooked endeavors. To this system must be added the availability of force and terror to make the hesitant fall in with the party line. More than half of the world lives under tyrannical regimes and has as much true freedom of logical choice as the galley slave on a Roman boat.

There are innumerable systems of logic, indeed, as many as were offered to the eager readers as objective interpretations of man's method of thinking. The fact of the matter is that man's method of thinking is no more than a reflector of man's brain power deeply involving the whole physiological body. As Baruch Spinoza stated in his *Ethics*, Body and Mind are one and the same thing, observed under two different attributes. It is easy to observe average man's reaction to certain given phenomena. In practical matters, for example, burnt children will shun the fire in China as well as in Timbuktu. In fact, the astonishing similarity of proverbs and other practical statements all over the globe, in primitive as well as modern times is prima facie evidence that men think alike—in matters of practical occurrences. Indeed man does not think; *It* thinks in man. All bodies think alike; we could not get along without such concurrence for a single month or day. Assuming we understand each other's language, were I to say to an Australian aborigine, "Go back," he would have no doubt what I meant; were I to say to a Tibetan shepherd, "Two cows and two more make four," he would have no problem comprehending this formula.

All this uniformity and simplicity of human verities disappears, however, when the natural mind of the people is deliberately confused by interested or scheming persons who set out to influence or dominate a group. Suddenly out from crevices of superstition or temples of worship appear adulterating elements of the mind, deliberately or foolishly spread to confuse citizens, strangers and servants into accepting unbelievable humbug as truth while casting truth to the winds as heretic or sinful.

No man was ever born without conception; no woman ever sprang full-grown from the forehead of a man or from the foam of seawater; no man came to this globe riding on the back of a bird, etc., etc. Yet such nonsense is imposed on the minds of children, over most of the world's three billion inhabitants, and kept active in the minds of the people by such vulgar threats as: Disbelief is heresy and heresy is sin.

Early and heavily imposed superstitions and confusions are not only of religious composition; much stronger are those of imperialistic, despotic or self-seeking origin. Invariably those pretentious untruths are offered to the public sweet-coated as "humanitarianism," "pacifism," "love for the poor," and so on. No one ever played the theme of pacifism more nauseatingly than most bloody tyrants. These, bent upon sitting on an Olympic throne, with sympathy for the poor, the ill, the dispossessed, the maltreated, the abused. The aspiring despot wishes to unite the people—of course, always under his or her generous and just scepter. Isabella united all of Spain upon the corpses of Jews, Moors and no few Iberians; Napoleon wanted to unite all of Europe under his self-made crown; Catherine did unite all the Russians and other blood-red tribes under her shameless skirt. Hitler wanted to unite all the pure races in a grand *Walpurgisnacht* pack of were-wolves and witches; Stalin drew himself up to the full height of his mediocrity and for a generation made the Kremlin into an antechamber of Lubjanka prison and the Siberian labor camps.

One must bear in mind that throughout the last seven thousand years of known history, the twenty large empires and hundreds of little empirettes were held together mainly by control of all major systems of communication. People were either confused into accepting the despot as a bene-volent big brother, terrorized into total frustration, fear and submission, or when necessary, bought by the all-powerful camarilla not only to accept the Devil's dictate but even to defend and propagandize it. Since time immemorial, the sup-pressors of the people, the Caesars, the Borgias, the Maos, the Alexanders, the Hitlers, the Pharaohs have managed to enslave the innocent, the people at work and at play, not only with the help of willing shamans and priests, but also with the help of eager scientists, artists, writers and greedy office-seekers. As the Hebrew sages said: Brother would betray brother to sit at the King's table. The masses were terrorized, but the elite were bought. Thousands of illustrious German artists and philosophers, scientists and clergymen sang the great chorale of "Hitler Forever," from Martin Heidegger to Gerhart Hauptmann and Reverend Ludwig Müller. Is it necessary to enumerate the many Russian "intellectuals" and artists who sang the sickening praise of Stalin, the Grand Executioner? And silent flows the Don carrying the bodies of tortured victims into the Black Sea.

It is hardly necessary to devise systems of logic, either as working models or for possible improvement. Logic is the functioning of the body; logic *is* the body in operation. You can as little change that as you can change the logic of a porpoise into that of a parrot or a donkey. The despoilers of the world know how man's mind works and they use this simple knowledge with the help of bought intelligentsia to pervert the people's thinking into hating nonexistent enemies and worshiping the devil himself. One little, but very old, perhaps the oldest, example of perennial hate: the Christian gospels teach the Christian children in a highly dramatized fashion of the bestial mutilation of the body of Jesus of Nazareth at the behest of "The Jews." So overwhelming is this tale of wanton cruelty and the Christian theologians' admonition to children and adult readers that the Lord will punish the Jews forever, disperse them over the earth, destroy Jerusalem, etc., that it was hardly necessary to tell the traumatized Christians specifically to hate the Jews. Perhaps two thousand years ago a Hebrew jury condemned the Jew Jesus. We have forgiven the Christians the killing of almost ten million Jews in two thousand years; they can not forgive us the killing of one. They have not yet stopped making new plays of the old horrible drama that makes Greeks, Romans,

106

Syrians and Egyptians into noble believers and the Jews, the makers of the great religions, into bloodthirsty pagans!

Our great problem, if we really wish for a better world, is not to peruse sundry texts in logic by well-meaning school teachers, but to stop the propaganda of hate. Stop anti-Semitism by extirpating the few dozen Jew-hating revolting lines from the New Testament. Stop the propaganda of the political mafias of the Communist empires by exposing them and their bridled helpers and helper's helpers. It is not the slow thinkers or the simple thinkers who have brought disaster to this world. It is the shrewd and the cunning who raise havoc on our little planet. Fight the real evildoers, not the dummies they set up for you to hate.

Hate is the father of all evil. Kill hate and the world will be good.

LOGODAEDALY

Logodaedaly is perhaps the greatest threat to philosophy. The inclination to creation and pursuit of word-labyrinths has beclouded the living problems of ethics from Aristotle to Husserl. Logodaedaly begins with the coining of multiple terms, preferably with Latin or Greek root. These new terms, only dimly interpreted, are then subdivided and made to relate to each other in newly proposed figures of relationship. Among the moderns, Hegel, Husserl and Heidegger are masters of the *imago*.

In matters of ethics, these and men of similar tendency enmeshed their power of judgment so intricately that neither they nor their diverse interpreters ever get to the point of answering the great but simple questions: what is goodness and what is morality? Then involvement in self-created jungles of *termini philosophici* brings forth a flurry of explanatory propositions where only a single sentence is expected and thus we find ourselves at the end of ten thousand years of moralizing with a hundred thousand books on ethics and not a single authentic and acceptable regulative for a moral life.

LOGOMACHY

Logomachy involving terminological, semantic and hierarchal battles has not ceased to trouble the fundamental issues of man's morality. In the Arianism of early Christianity; in the Scholastic schism; in the separationism of ecclesiastic orders; among the branches of Islam, the Sunnites, the Shiites, the Ismailis; in the midst of scores of Hindu ritualistic variations—sight is lost of the fundamental issue: where is genuine goodness in this torrent of doctrinism? Moralistic logomachy has so deeply infiltrated morality that even the religions prophetically revealed as new orders of human conduct carry on their church activities without even an attempt at bringing goodness into the life of man. The Christians are preoccupied with devotional differences in accepting Jesus and/or Holy Ghost,, the Moslems in weighing the proper exclusiveness of Mohammed, the Hindus in tenaciously holding on to caste and karma and so on.

With all this logomachy the Christian churches have been almost totally blind, or shall we say nearsighted, in the face of war, despotism, prejudice and hate right at the church gates. The Hindus have consistently kept their animals in greater comfort than their Untouchables, and for the Moslems the idea of *Jihad,* the never-ceasing war against disbelievers, has never ceased to be a paramount preoccupation. Somehow the vines of logomachy have so entwined the tree of life that the fruits of true morality, freedom and justice, were given to the common man not by men of the cloth but by men of the pen and the forge.

LOVE

Love seeks togetherness; love is togetherness. But love is a most dangerous word. It says so much and means nothing.

At the height of the Himmler massacres in Europe, Pope Pius XII issued repeated utterances on the need for love. These admonitions were so couched that Christian Europe, Catholic as well as Protestant, interpreted them as a lesson for the Allies! The French under Pétain continued to hunt up Jewish women and children to supply Eichmann; so did the Italians, Hungarians, Poles and others tuned in on the Vatican.

To the Jews, a Christian speaking of love is like a tiger growling psalms. Twice have I come across Christian expressions of love that sounded sincere. Once in a diary a contemporary of Montaigne cited a Dominican monk supervising the burning of Jews in Spain, who exclaimed, "I love these Jews; they burn much quicker than our own heretics." The second sincere expression of admiration for the Jews came from a German officer of the Nazi execution squad who gently praised the Jews he was putting to death in Babi Yar for dying silently with a prayer while his other victims, the Gypsies, made a great noise with laments and wailings.

In the history of executions of ten million Jews at the hands of Christian persecutors, not a single case comes to mind where love conquered Christian bestiality. However, Christian love always appears when it comes to the punishment of the Christian killers by some secular authority. Even the death-silent Vatican raised its voice and wrung its hands to save the jailed Nazi torturers from the arms of justice. Eichmann himself received a saving passport from the Vatican to escape his judges.

Love is not an element of ethics. Mother-love is basic, but not to ethics. Filial love is basic, but loving sons and loving parents, loving friends and lovers in marriage have broken and do break every precept of morality, social consideration and have offended the very basis of decency and the humanitarian code. The despotic, lecherous and murderous Czarina Catherine II was a loving mother; Napoleon Bonaparte, the Corsican guttersnipe who rose to the throne by blood and deceit, plunging Europe into bloodshed and misery, was a most loving brother; Alexander, perhaps the most deliberately brazen military adventurer in history, was proverbial for his love of friends and comrades; Stalin was forlorn and despondent when his first wife died, but his years of power were years of incomprehensible bestiality against foes and mere citizens.

Love of one's own is not a virtue; it is neither characteristic of a man's personality nor pertinent to social consideration. Cats and dogs love their own; birds and ants are staunch and loving providers. And miserable human monsters are as often as not lovers in their own circles. In ethics it matters not what you do to yourself or for yourself and your animal circle. It matters what you do or fail to do beyond your egocentric horizon. It is only in relation to acts and attitudes beyond the personal realm that a man's ethical caliber can be adjudicated. Who cares if you love father or children, brother or wife, or the Good Lord Himself, if you deal with fellow man in kindness, tolerance and generosity? Some say they love Jesus with all their hearts, but they are brutal to the black man across the tracks, or the Jew in his funny synagogue, or the fellow low on the totem pole of success, or the foreigner across the river. They claim to love God but they hate like the Devil; rather, they love the Devil and act like human beings.

When I hear the word love, I run for cover. Alexander invaded Greece out of love for Macedonia and butchered ten thousand Greeks in Thebes because they refused to join in his attack on Persia. He plundered Asia out of love for Greece. Caesar fell upon Gaul out of love for Rome and then upon Britain out of love for Gaul and then he fell upon Rome out of love for Caesar. Lenin fell upon the White Russians out of love for the Socialists and then upon the Socialists out of love for the Bolsheviks. Stalin fell upon the Bolsheviks out of love for the Russians; then he fell upon the Russians and sent three million to death and fifteen million to Siberian labor camps. Finally he fell upon his friends out of love for Stalin. All the despots on all the continents are forever loving peace and loving their citizens and thus they turn to conquest and oppression.

The word love from the lips of preachers and politicians, teachers and poets is no more than a dramatic gesture. There is no substance to it. The precept, love thy enemy, is ludicrous in a world where people hate their neighbors. Much wiser would it be just to forget the word love away from the family and tribal hearth, and make a sincere appeal to all concerned for fairness, tolerance and kindness. Let's just love father and mother, brother and sister, husband and wife; as for the rest of the world, let's be good to them and compassionately helpful.

MAN

Man's position in this universe is small. Some little people make big talk about man's supreme position on this globe and they expostulate about "mastering" the planets and the galaxies and all that lies beyond. Take another look, a good look, and what do you see? A billion creatures digging a miserable living out of Mother Earth—chewing her grain, biting her fruit, butchering her animals and dumping scum all over her rivers, forests and meadows. Where are the masters of this tiny corner of the universe? Killing and scheming, scheming and killing; neighbor bleeding neighbor; land hating land and furtively preparing to bury the other in its own dung. And the prime achievement of all the action is little more than a mountain of monstrous bombs readied for the next war.

Man's position in this world is low, way down at the bottom. Man is the great killer; he uses words to confuse his adversaries, hateful lies to pervert youth, and knowledge to prepare instruments of destruction. Every ten years another war breaks out; in between there are many little wars. War is man's main occupation. It takes most of his resources, attention and planning. Man's position in this universe is little indeed; and that little is evil.

MARXIST ANTI-SEMITISM

The shadow of Soviet anti-Semitism grows steadily wider and deeper. The anti-Semitism that was described by former Soviet chief Nikita Khrushchev as a malevolent project of the late Party Secretary Joseph Stalin turned out to be a widespread—one can say global—characteristic of Marxist

Leftists of the previous and present centuries. Indeed, the anti-Semitic fundamentalism of Adolf Hitler's National Socialism differed little from the anti-Semitism of Soviet Russia today. Both Adolf Hitler and Joseph Stalin and their followers drank from the same fountain of Jew-hatred, Karl Marx's *Probleme Zur Judenfrage.*

I find it necessary, indeed essential, to state that Karl Marx was not a Jew, neither at the age of six when he was converted by his parents to the Protestant faith, nor at any time in his adult life. The parents of Karl Marx were born Jews; they both became converts to the Lutheran church—that very same Luther who demanded that ". . . the homes, the belongings and the Talmuds of the Jews be burned and they be kept in befitting servitude to the Christian people." In the middle of the nineteenth century when Karl Marx wrote the vicious essay *Problems of Judaism,* racial theories were not dominant and if a man changed his religion, he was accepted without hesitancy or reserve. The boy Karl Marx never in his life had any training in Judaism or even true knowledge of the Jewish faith, a lack of information which is woefully evident in his later writings. Raised by a mother and father who were renegades to their ancient faith, he heard and later read the typical anti-Semitic interpretations of Judaism for which Luther's church was renowned. Who can forget this horrible exclamation by Martin Luther: "If a Jew refuses to accept the divinity of the Lord Jesus, apprehend him and cut his tongue out from the back of his neck." Such statements of Luther poisoned the religious atmosphere of the young Karl Marx, who in his first book of significance painted the following portrait of the Jewish religion:

Money is the jealous God of Israel;
To the Jew, sex is an object of commerce;
The Jew has only contempt for philosophy, art and history;
The foundation of the Jewish religion is selfishness;
The object of the Jews' worship is usury;

113

The Jew by his money manipulations decides the fate of Europe;

The Jew considers himself a member of a separate nation, a "Chosen People."

Looking at the applied principles of National Socialism and Communist statecraft, we find that both these movements endorse almost completely the anti-Semitic theses of Karl Marx. Like the Hitler regime, Soviet Russia punishes attempts to leave one's country by death; self-determined migration is considered a capital crime. Like Hitler's Germans, the Soviet citizens have no right to assemble, no right to free speech or free pen, no right to print or draw or paint or teach or preach freely. Over every one of these activities hangs the noose of Leningrad or the bullet of Lubjanka prison. As in Hitler's National Socialism, in the Soviet Union and its satellites as well, the whole administration, or what is called the government, is appointed by a camarilla, a mafia of political "ins." The people have no hand in the election of any public official of any significance. This practice is a reversion to total absolutism as in the feudal eras. Hitler compelled the Jews to add the co-name Sarah or Israel to their names to separate them from the other citizens. The Soviet government persistently publishes the Jewish co-name next to the Russian name of the Jewish inhabitants. They also mark all basic work papers and every single passport held by a Jew with a special stamp "Jew," in addition to the province or state of origin. Such segregation is applied only to Jews.

Hitler destroyed all Jewish houses of worship; Soviet Russia shut down all Jewish houses of worship save only a handful as showplaces for tourists. The National Socialists burned all Jewish books and ritual objects, prohibiting by threat of death their distribution; the Soviet government destroyed or otherwise eliminated all Jewish literature, all books of Jewish history, religion or cultural aspirations. They also forbade the use, sale or distribution of any Jewish religious articles as "Zionist propaganda," such distribution an offense

114

punishable by death. National Socialism engaged in repeated publication of vile accusations against the Jewish people, illustrated by defamatory cartoons of citizens of the Jewish faith. Soviet Russia, where all publications are in the hands of government agencies, has printed and given away hundreds of thousands of booklets by notorious anti-Semites such as Kichko, Ivanov, Mayatsky, Shevtsov. The National Socialist movement had prepared in its early stages a complete register of all Jewish and half-Jewish citizens for later "action." The very same system was inaugurated by Stalin and continued by the present administration of Brezhnev, Kosygin and Podgorny with obvious intent. In dealings with the West, the Hitler government was in the habit of substituting for the word Jews such synonyms as internationalists, Zionist bankers, international financiers, alien colonialists, and so on, and referred to the "New York-Tel Aviv axis." Similar synonyms have been and are being used by the Soviet government with the obvious purpose of covering the stench of medieval anti-Semitism with the perfume of refined terminology. Like the National Socialists, the Soviet government does not hesitate to use obsolescent church prejudice to impugn the loyalty of the Jews by saying that they engage in their synagogues in shabby business deals to deprive the honest Christian of his earnings. Indeed, the vile shabbiness of National Socialist propaganda is reborn in the so-called anti-Zionism of Soviet Russia's political mafia.

The National Socialists had a special medical department, the specific duty of which was detention for various experimental and punitive purposes. The Soviet administration has a similar section connected with their secret service, whose chief duty is to apprehend recalcitrant citizens, Jews and such, and set them straight. Some of the patients leave these institutions rehabilitated; others, hard cases, are transferred to more primitive detention places. Concentration camps, which abounded in Siberia during the Stalin era and are flourishing anew these last ten years, enjoyed a considerable popularity in Russia before their equivalents appeared further west during the Hitler regime. In all these camps, Soviet and Nazi alike, starvation diets were introduced, the purpose of which was to replace outright execution by ax, bullet or hanging with slow starvation and isolation. In both lands, Nazi and Soviet, the Jews were brutally chosen for victimization.

The Hitler-Stalin pact of 1939 shook the world because of the callous and cynical attitude of the two alleged enemies. The adoption of the Marxist anti-Semitic governmental policy now practiced in the Soviet Union is no less cynical and no less brutal than the Stalin-Hitler military alliance at the beginning of World War II. It was Karl Marx who believed that the only way the world could emancipate itself from the Jews was by cleansing itself of Judaism in all its implications—a world without Jews. The goal was the same for the German National Socialists and the Soviet Communists.

MASS

A viewpoint does not become better because many subscribe to it.

MENTAL CHECKUP

Have a mental checkup at least twice a year. The ancient Hebrews had it at the beginning of the year. Weigh your deeds and weigh your words. Have you blindly followed the party lines or schemes of corrupt self-seeking politicos or operators? Have you refused to stand up and speak out from opportunistic motivation? Have you openly admitted when you were culpably wrong?

Who never changes his mind has no mind to change. There are not too many chances given to man to turn courageous and honest and unbiased. Don't miss them! Soon it is too late. It is almost too late now. This is a short life; make it at least count by its depth and conviction.

MICROSCOPE VS. TELESCOPE

How very much has microscopy done for mankind in medicine, agriculture and other fields of productive scientific endeavor and how little has the telescope contributed to the welfare of mankind! Perhaps some of the philosophers of the seventeenth century were right to discourage Galileo Galilei and others in their ardent efforts to promote sky research! The present space science flurry with its immense expenditures has similarly found hard critics who see in most of the space activities an unpardonable waste of money which in our times is so scarce for direct health and welfare development.

MIND

The mind works along various avenues. These avenues are not necessarily connected or even parallel. A great psychologist for instance may have a sound understanding of anthropology, yet a segment of his mind may be filled to the brim with spiritual nonsense from "automatic writing" to "secret orders from other worlds." Thomas Edison, a man of eminent scientific clarity, on other wavelengths of his brain fabricated a machine in the hope of talking to the dead. Karl Marx, who penetrated the layers of our social structure, was himself on certain thought levels victim of violent racial prejudices against the Jews and their religion. He spoke of all Jews as usurers and money-mad capitalists although in his time ninety percent of the European Jews and almost one hundred percent of the Oriental Jews were destitute peddlers and petty artisans. In dealing with so-called great men, it is important to distinguish which of their mind avenues are high, which low.

MIRACLES

Any man attempting to deny the existence of miracles or the divine interposition in the natural course of events I

117

would consider foolish, as there are many thousands of witnesses throughout history attesting to their verity. Of course, as the centuries roll by, the various religions are getting more and more hesitant not only to canonize but even to accept or tolerate miracle makers. The Protestants and the Mohammedans lean toward restricting miracles to the scriptural events. The Romans relate a great number of vouched-for miracles such as that of Emperor Vespasian, who healed a sick man and a lame one in Alexandria by the laying on of hands in front of a crowd of onlookers; the kings of England traditionally had the power to cure their subjects of scrofula by mere touch, and here, too, the irrefutable witnesses are available. The Greeks attest to a myriad of miraculous happenings: the god Zeus lying with Alcmene (the Greek gods seem to have been compulsive players of the game of love in manifold ways and byways) made the welcome night last twenty-four hours instead of twelve. The greatest miracle befell Achilles, who was addressed by his horse Xanthus, and foretold that he would die before Troy.

I could go on enumerating a thousand times a thousand miracles occurring in Asia, Africa, Europe and America, all reported by reliable writers and many heavily documented. On this continent miracles seem to have flourished in the last century. One man alone, Joseph Smith, a New York farmer, founded the Mormon Church on a bevy of miracles, beginning with the hidden golden plates of scripture and ending with his truly miraculous power to bring about salvation of women by taking them to bed as auxiliary wives.

There are some who regard all miracles, including the biblical ones, as so much fairy tale or humbug. I can't quite accept this supposition. I say rather, what is the moral value of a miracle, granting it occurred? If a leper stretches out his hand to the image of an accredited saint, in supplication and true reverence, and he is cured, then by what peculiar justice are all other lepers left to rot? If one little girl is brought back to life by her mother's devout genuflecting, by what peculiar justice are a million other children sent to their grave? If one possessed by a demon is exorcised of his mania, by what peculiar justice are the herds of other maniacs left in their chains and terror? If one blind man can have his eyes freed from disease, why not the rest? Why not the rest?

No one in his right mind will say that the lame, the blind, the ill, the insane, the dead upon whom the miracle fell were more deserving than the others or that one sick child's soul was more precious than the souls of sick children at large. We must therefore conclude that while miracles may be true, they do not occur by wise providence, but rather by accident, and are therefore no evidence of the miracle-worker's morality.

What does it mean when an itinerant preacher can stretch out his arm and let a poisonous snake bite into it? What good is a faith that perhaps acts as an antidote? What does it mean if another saint can restore a man's eyesight with a bit of spit? It enhances the performer, but the remaining million blind continue to grope in the dark. What value is it that a sublime Yogi can suck in water with his anus or swallow his own tongue? Or that a Hindu can stay buried alive for a week or a saintly Zen priest can hang from a tree branch for a fortnight by one arm? Or that a Buddha makes a seemingly dead child come to life by touching its forehead? What good is all that if the continent of India's dead will not arise?

Miracles prove nothing, nothing at all. I would like to see the miracle of the great religions making their billions of followers stop killing the Jews, or the Gypsies, or each other, for that matter! At the time when the great Christian church was compiling its saints' almanacs and the calendars of miracles, it was helping launch the Crusades, which were nothing but murderous campaigns of conquest with the Cross on the left shoulder and the Devil beneath. The church traveled with Columbus, Cortez, Pizarro and the others on the great western treks of discovery, with conversion as pretext and gold-greed as the real motive. The churches were silent, very silent, when their lords robbed Africa of its best sons, who were hunted like wild game and packed into dirty old holds as you would ship cattle, to be sold as slaves to other Christians. These defenders of the Christian faith never ceased to have their sport with the "killers of God's Son" by torture racks and the final flame.

And all the while the Christian literature is stuffed with tales of miracles and legends of the astonishing talents of the sainted, from understanding the tongues of birds to licking the pus off the open wounds of lepers, from praying for months at a stretch to keeping silent for years, sitting for a lifetime on top of a pillar, and sundry other astonishing miracles.

I say, dispense with all miracles! Let us have some true deeds of kindness—simple, honest, and continuing kindness to all people, even to those who, they say, killed God. Why should my grandson be marked a devil and a Jew and a Zionist because two thousand years ago, they say, a hundred Jews condemned another Jew to death for pretentiousness?

Let the churches preach ordinary peace to all the ordinary people. Let us cut out the self-praising fables of the miracles of the saints. Even if they were all true, they mean nothing to the world. Let the Christian churches work not toward their self-aggrandizement, but toward the one great people's miracle: peace to all mankind.

MISERY

Misery for man can originate with nature or human malevolence. For millions of years, man suffered mainly from "acts of God" such as pestilence, earthquake, flood, fire and injury. Then for the last fifty thousand years, the natural tribulations have been outweighed by those inflicted by man's inhumanity to man. Hordes of people have been summoned by usurpers to do battle against neighbors, cutting them, stabbing them, starving them, parching them, blinding them.

120

How small appear the evils of nature compared with those brought about by people against people! Warriors were roused by self-seeking prophets to invade the grazing lands nearby, driving shepherds into the desert where they, in turn, decimated the ranks of oasis settlers, cutting off their hands or putting out their eyes, leaving the bleeding to scorching agony. Caliphs with the curved sword cut out an empire dedicated to Islam from the Atlantic across Africa and Eurasia to the Pacific of Polynesia. Generations later, Crusaders waded in the blood of Moslems from the Atlantic to the Jordan River in the service of the gentle Jew Jeshu son of Joseph, whom they revered as God. All of these gods in the war cries of wild horsemen, all those holy symbols, were spattered with blood of the innocent.

And is it better now? Now the barbarism is committed by armadas remote in air or water. The sword and spear have been replaced by bomb, grenade and invisible missile, and the new god is communism or fascism or some such divinity as peripheral as Allah or Jesus or Caesar. What matters it? The banner changes but in command are the very same greedy upstarts and never-die-outs who have driven man against man always. Man cannot live in peace, not because of the gods, not because of differences in faith or reason, but because of the insatiable lust for power of a few monstrous despots and their kin or clique. Those who bombarded Warsaw and Coventry differ little from those who burned Jerusalem or Carthage. And those who cut off the head of an opponent in Berlin, or fired a shot into the back of a prisoner's head in Moscow are only continuing the grisly work of the Mongolian and Egyptian warlords of other centuries.

Man's indescribable misery is not to be laid upon ignorance or lack of religion, but rather upon the connivance and cruelty of the few who make a mockery of humanity, who use the name of the Lord as a battle cry and the faith of the gullible to inflame hate, murderous hate, against their victims. Power lust of the few is at the root of all the great evils; the rest is low cunning and deviltry. From the Roman

121

warlords to the Russian and German party leaders, runs a chain of invasions and savage destructions allegedly to save humanity. You cannot save humanity by the sword, nor can you build peace under the aegis of criminals.

MONASTICISM

Monasticism is a way of life implying isolated singularity. The motivations for self-abnegation are manifold; we have among all cultural groups occasional flights into isolation by the frightened, the misanthropic, the impotent, the disillusioned and, of course, the fanatically devout. Already in the early centuries of Buddhism, Judaism, Christianity, and other faiths we find legends and chronicles of dedicated believers who fled a neighborhood which they fanatically judged to be sinful, heathen, tempting or an obstacle to a good life hereafter. These men took to the desert as hermits (from the Greek *eremos,* lonely), the forest, or even climbed a pillar—in Greek, *stylos,* thus gaining the sobriquet "Stylites."

Be they hermits or anchorites ("withdrawn men" from the Greek word *anachorein,* to withdraw), they were monastic in the true sense. Buddhists, Hebrews or Christians, they lived for themselves, retreating to cave or desert rock, tree or lean-to, exposing themselves deliberately in inadequate and coarse covering, self-attached chains or total uncleanliness. As great as their suffering undoubtedly was, they bore it with equanimity, even exhilaration, since their faith in a glorious hereafter was an ecstatic recompense for *terra dolorosa.*

There is no morality, of course, in personal suffering for one's own expected beatification. It is a form of refined self-centeredness that would make a man drop his family and social responsibilities and desert his work, worry and civic duties to hide in the desert or dark of the forest like a mole, giving over his body to eating and sleeping and his mind to reciting prayers. Still, while monasticism is ethically not

122

meritorious, in itself it is harmless and enables the weak, the frightened and the poor in soul plagued by religious superstition to escape whatever they are dreading.

In later centuries Buddhism and Christianity, but not Judaism, developed a large movement of cenobites, monks who obviously desired their monastic existence to be tempered by company and communal activities. Reference to those large orders and institutions with their abbeys, gardens, schools, hospitals, libraries, and vineyards, as "monastic" is hardly accurate. They deserve at best the title of sexually segregated brotherhoods, bound by certain religious and work observances. These "monastic" congregations do take the vow of chastity, poverty and obedience, but theirs cannot be considered an existence of isolation.

Some of the vows of these men-communities, such as perennial silence and extensive prayer recital, are a heavy obligation, but I do not feel that as such the principles upon which these orders are founded should be given moral evaluation, although some of their welfare activities are as helpful as those of the secular agencies. Ethically it has no meaning whatever if monks carry out even their useful chores in a state of sleeplessness (the Acoemetae); keep up a chain of never-ending prayers and wear hair shirts (Capuchins); humiliate themselves in horrible penances for alleged infractions against the seven deadly sins; commit each other to periodical or permanent silence; neglect the care of their bodies and so forth. The same, of course, applies to religious orders of women. Historically we never had women hermits or anchorites. But we do have a great many religious orders offering a life of segregation from the male and family. Significantly, the churches refer to the inhabitants of their respective monasteries as nuns (from the Latin *nonna, old woman*).

There is no virtue in celibacy, ascesis, physical neglect or worldly indifference in hope of a magnificent hereafter. The motivation here is entirely egotistic. Even if it were a wise choice—perhaps it is—it is taken to elevate no one but oneself!

MONUMENTS

Streets and parks the world over are infested with statues and other memorials to some of the worst political and social criminals. From the pharaohs to Hitler, from Genghis Khan to Stalin, why should the memory of the great oppressors and despots of the people be perpetuated? It is time to break all monuments to the vain and vicious "leaders" into rubble and bury the rubble in the sand. Rip their portraits and break their plaques. Fill the vacant spots with likenesses of the true men of leadership who more often than not were victims of the oppressor.

How is our youth to learn the difference between good and evil, justice and inhumanity, if in all its reading and learning it comes across the laurel-wreathed images of historic monsters like Caesar or Tamerlane or Stalin or Hitler in positions of honor? Let them, the young, despise and hold in contempt the self-seeking despot, be he king or noble, czar, führer, or "chairman," and teach them to hold in esteem only those who worked for the people, not at the bloody expense of the people.

MOSES

Moses was not the creator of the Jewish faith. Unlike the other religions, the Hebrew faith is the Word of God. Moses was one of the great interpreters. Noah and Abraham were interpreters of the Hebrew faith and had left to the people a covenant. For a thousand years before Moses, there was a Torah of the Jewish nation to which the Jews even in Egyptian slavery adhered. They kept the covenant and never left it. Moses was not the creator of the Hebrew Torah; he was its great defender and interpreter.

124

MUFFLER

The Russians have always been quite vocal about their discoveries. But they have not yet boasted of a new form of psychoanalytic treatment: Take a talking scientist into the mental clinic and in a few weeks out comes a silent scientist.

MURDER

Murder is still the dominant topic of fiction writers. Next in popularity is sexual involvement with perverse undertones. What revolting intimacy: morbid or sordid literati in the pay of decadence.

NAPOLEON

Napoleon obtained nothing but fame, the twin sister of infamy. The public often fails to distinguish which is which.

NEUROSIS

During the last hundred years, it has become literary as well as parlor fashion willfully to extend some of the traditional medical terms for somatic and functional nervous disorders to persons showing emotional or intellectual peculiarities. Under the influence of the Viennese neurologist Sigmund Freud, schools and groupings of psychoanalytic interpreters were developed, each of them eager to interpret, evaluate and curatively direct alleged and real neural aberrations.

Freud himself, who until his last years frowned upon the physicians arrogating to themselves the practice of psychoanalysis, concentrated on finding the sexual impulse as sole and deep-rooted motivating agent, a somewhat one-sided protagonism of Spinoza's definition of the Lust for Pleasure. Fanatically looking for the causal factors, inhibitions, deviations and other symptoms of emotional conflict in the first years of a child's life, when infantile sexual drives are frustrated, Freud, himself a pitiful victim of sexual confusion in childhood, felt strongly that he had found the key to compulsion and complexes in the toilet and eating habits of infants and their parent relationship. The Greek mythology of Oedipus, the theories of his teacher Charcot about the subconscious—these and his father's second marriage to an attractive young woman played undoubtedly a tremendous part in the formation of his dramatic sex and dream theories.

This is not the place to present statistics—whatever little

126

is available—germane to the subject of psychoanalytic cure. Certain is that, especially in this country, whole armies of physicians by merely going personally through the process of psychoanalysis, refer to themselves as psychiatrists, a term until the last three decades used exclusively as the designation of specialists dealing with neural disorders or psychotics. Droves of other professionals, with or without diverse degrees of education, joined an obviously lucrative field of psychotherapy, using in the main Freudian techniques of dream analysis in years-long "treatment." As we are still living in an era when the etiology of schizophrenia, paranoia and manic depression is totally unknown, it is only natural that all these dynamic therapists could not and would not respect the ill-defined borders between psychosis and neurosis, between behavior neurosis and plain odd behavior.

It is interesting to note that in countries such as Russia, Freudian psychoanalysis is criminally prosecuted as fraud, along with fortune telling and astrology. In most other parts of Europe, such as Italy, Spain, Germany, France, it is controlled and restricted and flagrant abuses are eliminated.

This, as I said before, is not the place to deal with the medical issues in neurasthenia, hysteria, hypochondria, and so on. We are here concerned with the moral aspects of psychoanalytic practice insofar as it tends toward pansexualism. The common psychoanalytic practice of seeking sexual motivation in all human endeavor, whether art, politics, literature, philosophy, social relationship, or family relationship, leads inevitably to the "patient" becoming fixated on sexual symbols in all ideas, concepts and relationships. Any affection is suspect; so is every sign of displeasure. Every slip in word or pen is automatically explained by its hidden sexual inference: the offering of a knife or fork, the hesitance at a door handle, the dropping of a shoe, the neglect to close a bag, the raising of a finger, the pouting of an infant—in brief, any and every gesture and word is sagely placed in its proper Freudian relationship to penis, anus and vagina. And of course the dreams—the opportunities offered there are a veritable treasure chest in the hands of an astute Freudian scientist.

After a few months, when the "patient" has acquired the lower strata of psychoanalytic terminology, both doctor and doctored wallow in nondescript mutual explanation of the true meaning of the dreams on the couch. To quote the most eminent Russian psychologist, Pavlov, it will take generations to discredit and finally eliminate the Freudian practice of psychoanalysis; fads blossom overnight but they are rather slow to fade entirely.

NEUTRALITY

Neutrality is rarely a virtue. More often than not it is a crime, the crime of indifference, the crime of escaping responsibility, of cowardice in the face of probable consequences, of a two-faced attitude which works both sides unbeknown to each other for personal advantage. Even states appear noncommitted, at least on the surface, while in reality they are strongly committed underground. Yugoslavia was neutral in the war between the Hungarian Republic and the forces of Khrushchev, while in reality it betrayed the Hungarian freedom fighters including the prime minister and thus enabled Russia to capture and execute the revolutionaries. Pope Pius XII protested his neutrality in the "conflict" between the Nazi regiments and Jewish refugee children and women, thus saving not the innocent but rather the face of the monstrous executioners.

History is replete with examples of pseudo-neutrality engendered either by political fears or political opportunism. Look out for the neutral; he may be more dangerous to you than the open enemy.

NEW IDEAS

New ideas are indeed rare. More often than commonly suspected, the latter-day gurus merely rebottle old prophetica and present the modern reader eager to drink from the new fountain no more than familiar vintage. India and its satellite California are especially blessed with dressed-up sages who diversify the grand simplicity of Hinduism and Buddhism by terminology that mistakes frills for profundity.

NEW TESTAMENT

It is a grave pity that this great collection of ancient Hebrew wisdom, spoken and written almost without exception by sages of Israel, is marred by latter-day church biographers, commentators and church fathers who deliberately interpolated accusations of deicide, blasphemy and downright bestiality allegedly practiced by God's chosen people. Although the Catholic Church, on whose shoulders the responsibility for this historic wrong, bitter wrong, rests, endeavored under the blessed Pope John XXIII to make amends, his successor unfortunately did not follow through in removing the Jew-condemning passages of the present-day editions of the New Testament. Every Christian child, Catholic or Protestant, absorbs with its earliest Sunday school lessons all of the one hundred and two ugly references to "the Jew" as they appear in the Greek scriptural texts. The original Hebrew scripts of the Jewish Apostles of Jesus, the Jew Paul and others are unknown to the western world. Most people assume that the intimates and evangelists of Jesus were Gentiles and that "the Jews" were the Master's torturers. In this sense, the early Roman Christian Church fathers speak of the Jews as "the Children of the Devil who do their Father's, the Devil's, lust." A hundred times in the New Testament the Jew is referred to as intrinsically evil, treacherous, greedy, and so on.

The Good Lord must have been awfully naive to select a Hebrew by flesh as His only begotten Son, and surround the Son with Hebrew apostles and evangelists, baptized by Jochanan, another Hebrew. The New Testament is a rich Hebraic work, written by Jews and for Jews only, since none of the other nations desired or expected a Messiah. The Roman bishops to show their gratitude to the Roman emperor interspersed innuendos and downright falsifications into this remarkable volume to smear the Jews and by reverse effect elevate the Romans, the butchers of antiquity, destroyers of Carthage, Alexandria, Athens and Jerusalem, thus making the debauched despots of Rome and Byzantium into noble benefactors of the son of Yahweh and his Israelite kinsmen into wanton god-killers.

It is time, high time, to cleanse the New Testament of these hateful, anti-Jewish blemishes, so that the richness of the Scriptures might serve all people of the world.

To the fourteen million Jews of today there is only one dominant concern before which all other issues and problems of the world recede into insignificance: how to stop the Christian from persecuting the Jew. The Christian child at home, in Sunday school, in church, is imbued with this hateful text and after ten years of "Biblical" brainwashing is not only totally indifferent to Jewish suffering but personally ready to participate in anti-Semitic outrages. The Christians of Germany and the rest of the European continent vied with each other to detect, apprehend and deliver Jewish children and women to the thousands of German concentration camps for gas murder and burning. But then again, Christian Europe has burned Jews for two thousand years. Popes did it; bishops did it; priests did it; and Luther made it part of his "theology" to burn everything Jewish.

These are facts which even the most opportunistic Christ clerics do not deny; however, they say, we are turning over a new leaf, the ecumenic leaf! What good is all that if the leaves they are turning still contain the same ugly references to the Jew as devil and so on? They read them softly now but the same malevolent lines that have incited ordinary Christian folk to pogroms all these centuries are at the root of the pogroms of today in Russia and Russian satellites.

There can be no peace for the Jew until the New Testament has been cleansed of all, but all, its anti-Semitic interpolation by ancient popism. When you confront a Christian cleric or theologian, asking, "Why do you say the Jews do the Devil's work?" he will answer you as cardinals and bishops have answered me: *"We* don't say it, God says it." True it is, God's Son is made to say "You Jews do the Devil's work." The ancient Christians slid the Old Testament to the bottom and superimposed a New Testament that is poisoned by a hundred interpolations by fine Roman hands to curry favor with Caesar who gave the Church an empire and to downgrade the Jews, who would never accept the old or the new Roman paganism.

So in the world of the New Testament there are two distinct peoples, the God-torturing Jews and the ever-loving Gentiles. Among those Gentiles rank the generous Roman procurator, Pilate, who belonged to the elite of Caesarian Rome which for a thousand years engaged in butcherous conquest of Mediterranean and adjacent lands, pillaging Athens, Carthage, Syracuse, Jerusalem, Alexandria. Those Nazis of antiquity become in the New Testament symbols of Gentileness, while God's chosen people from whom he took His Son, are God-killers. But God paid the Jews back by having the Gentile Titus burn Jerusalem, rape their women, enslave and disperse their children and nail them to crosses by the thousands in front of the crumbling walls of the Holy City. Thus reads the book made up by the pontiffs of Rome to teach the wide world love, faith and charity. It is for others to say how far the love effort of Rome's Christianity has succeeded. To us Jews it has been a constant call for terror against our people. Not a single decade has passed from the days of the ferociously anti-Semitic Church Fathers to Pius XII, when the Jews have not been beaten, burned and bled in the name of Christianity at the hands of Christians.

I suppose that, after the surfeit of Jewish blood during World War II and the demise of Pius XII, the Catholic Church with the Protestant splinter groups following rather hesitatingly were ready to forgive the Jewish people their being persecuted for two thousand years. But—the clerics would never really consent to giving up that inspiring drama

131

of the Godless Jews torturing and finally murdering God. In a final resolve, the Vatican decided to forgive the victims of Christian hate and declare: Not all Jews were or are guilty!

But the play must go on! Not a line, not an iota may be changed. The Play of Crucifixion, the first copy of which dates to the fourth century, must remain intact. Its one hundred and two murderous references to the Jews as obstinate pagans pressing for the mutilation and death of the Jew Jesus, these hateful references to all Jews of the world, past, present and to come, *must* remain Holy Script. So while with one hand outstretched the Christian churchmen offer awkward apologies for their inspired massacre of Jewish children, women and men over the centuries, with the other hand they point a huge accusing finger at the Jews as the torturers of the Jesus from Nazareth!

We all know and they all know that as long as the Christian children grow up under such perverted teachings, they will develop into the very same anti-Semitic fanatics that their ancestors did. The Greek Orthodox churches of today are poisoning the minds of Russian children as effectively as the Catholic and Protestant churches of Germany did a generation ago and the French Christians of today are as indifferent to Jewish fate as those of Marshal Pétain were. Bible Jew-hate is at the root of all anti-Semitism. The Christian church created Jew-hate and made it part and parcel of its theology. There is no Christianity without Jew-hate and all anti-Semitism is attributable directly or indirectly to the Christian Church.

Unless the one hundred and two anti-Semitic lines are removed from the "Holy Scripture," there will be no peace for Israel. The fate of a nation hangs on the sanctity of five-score ancient Roman interpolations. The rest is all just talk!

NOBILITY

We still have in our Western world ludicrous and pic-ayune persons who run about from horse race to gambling casino, from nightclub to beach resort and even to public assemblies and civic halls, calling themselves princes, counts, dukes, majesties, lords, barons, khans, and the like. There is nothing to them but a bit of faded heritage. If the young and those who never grow responsible would take a closer look at history, they would turn away in horror, in disgust from the stench and crime of the "aristocratic" past. One should, and if knowledgeable, would associate these obsolete ribalds of a sickly aristocracy with the actual palace dwellers of not so long ago, with all their revolting bestiality, greed and murderous oppressiveness. So knowing, one scarcely would defer to these living freeloaders of a reeking purple past as princes, lords and so on, but rather deal with them in word and deed as he would with descendants of Jesse James, Jack the Ripper or Blackbeard the pirate.

Unfortunately quite a few of our dollar or screen histo-rians find it advantageous to cater to the morbid cult of ex-tinct royalty. They keep on writing to a forgetful or ignorant public of the vainglorious past of this dungeonous aristocracy with affectionate camouflage and endearing sentimentality which could nohow be falser!

NOISE

There are those who mistake noise for action.

NOVELS

Isn't it peculiar that so many novels are given over to the lives and issues of young, very young, people? Puerile trivialities are drawn out before the eyes of the reader as if on this globe with its teeming billions it mattered whether Jack gets to mate with Anne or Jane winds up with John or

Mark. Where are the great novels of men and women at the mature and ripe ages when issues are deeper and more profound? Life is as exciting among the veterans as among the beginners. Perhaps the late flowers are more precious than the first.

NUDISM

Nudism is not immoral; it is inhumanly cruel. It excludes the crippled, the underdeveloped, the overdeveloped, the one-legged and the one-armed, the burned and wounded, the scarred, ailing and otherwise afflicted from society. For centuries, men of compassion have striven for the physically disadvantaged to be accepted at work and play as full equals. Means have been found or devised to make the one-legged walk and the one-armed become handy. Why forsake all empathy so that a bunch of frisky juveniles or elderly voyeurs can have a fling at exhibitionism?

Primitive tribes of old and of today who don't share our moralistic attitude nonetheless have been covering their genitals and points of bodily elimination for sake of safety and protection from insect life. The human body, by all means, may it be free. But human outlets of canalization, as all savages know, had best be covered. The battle is not worth the loincloth.

OLD AGE

Not all parts of a man die at the same rate. Indeed, we are forever renewing and forever disintegrating, like nature itself.

Old age begins when you are no longer concerned with what to put into the world but only with what you get out of the world. Old is only he who lost interest in tomorrow.

PACIFIST

A pacifist is not the man afraid of fighting, but the one dedicated to peace. The men who led their people against tyrants chose war over submission. They wanted peace for their families and comrades and not tranquil subservience. They preferred the sword to the chains. Kowtow is not a noble trait; if we are not ready to block despotism, we are not pacifists, just cowards.

PARASITE

Perhaps some centuries hence man will cease being a parasite on animal life. We scorn people and creatures that sponge on others, yet man is parasite par excellence. Last year, traveling on a Moroccan road, I passed a great goat herd grazing on a hill; a peasant appeared, grabbed one of the kids, cut its warm throat with a knife and dragged it into his hut. This Moroccan, as well as a million other herders and farmers, consider all, but all, animate things except man as their food, their clothing, their pleasure. They bleed the animals to death, then skin, sear and devour them; they steal the milk of those beasts, pull the hide off for covering. They have a whole body of science on how to use, abuse and increase the yield from animal life.

The religion of the Hebrews makes some restrictions: you may not boil an infant animal in the milk of its mother; you must kill an animal in a prescribed "painless manner;" you may not eat the flesh of pigs (probably because it tastes too much like human flesh and its parts such as heart, liver, kidneys, etc., look so very like those of man). Many cannibalistic tribes in the South Pacific have in olden days referred to humans as "long pigs." The Hebrew faith seems to indicate a disdain for or diffidence about eating the bodies of living creatures and perhaps for that reason forbids the eating of animals that live off other creatures, such as bear, or fox or shark.

While the Hebrew precepts are far from satisfactory, they suggest that to the soul of pious man the massacre of living creatures and gorging on their corpses is reprehensible. Man in his history of a million years has learned much about how to increase the yield of animal flesh, but has adapted nothing from his discoveries in agriculture and biochemistry to save animal flesh from being devoured by people.

PARTY

It is pitiful that so many sensible persons feel that they must always deride their party opponents and praise their party colleagues. My party, right or wrong—that is wrong.

PATRONS OF LITERATURE

Stalin, Hitler and Mussolini had more books dedicated to them than any other three persons in history. The charisma of office!

PEACE!

Peace! is an ancient Hebrew form of greeting. In modern times it often is a disarming appeal to the enemy population. The Nazis succeeded in making peace devotees of the French Socialist regime of Léon Blum. When France was thus pacified and disarmed, the Nazi armies jumped them. Peace never had more emphatic mongers than Hitler and Stalin. When their neighbors threw arms and caution to the wind, the peace protagonists fell upon them; Belgium, Holland, Denmark, Norway and of course France were stunned dupes in this peace game. Preach peace to your adversaries and preparedness to your own people, a proven road to conquest.

Beware of the peacemonger; he can be more dangerous than the warmonger. In view of the peacemonger's past record, it may not be so peculiar that those who carry the loud banner of peace today are given to arson, mayhem, assassination, kidnapping and other forms of violence.

PENANCE

Penance is the way of a transgressor to buy back innocence and grace by acceptance of temporal punishment. Churches of many denominations lean toward the sacred discipline of penance as it seems to strengthen the hand of spiritual order, but the belief that contrition of the penitent, combined with abject confession of venial and even mortal sins, will purify man's soul and prevent repetition of malfeasance is unjustified.

Penance is generally submitted to by the remorseful who feel sorrow, not for the victim of their transgression, but rather for themselves. It offers them escape from a troublesome conscience by wiping the slate of sin clean and securing an open door to the beatitudinous hereafter by such penitential exercises as prostrations, fasting, prayer, flagellation and minor deprivations of luxuries. Of course, much of what the penitent confesses to and is absolved from by many religions as sin is ethically meaningless; no punishment from either ecclesiastic or secular authorities is warranted for masturbation and other sexual abuses, envious feelings, heretical utterances, common fornication, failure to observe rituals or dietary precepts, and so on. Acts that do not affect the welfare of other persons are neither moral nor immoral, but, at worst, foolish or unhealthy, never sinful. To do penance for personal failings or feelings is a bargain made rather foolishly since no church or group can assure grace in the hereafter as reward for saying a thousand paternosters or making vows of abstinence.

Much of what is called sin is irrelevant, misnamed and

no public issue. What is really sinful, however, is the suppression of freedom, the harming of weaker neighbors, selfish arrogance toward neighbors, the hurting and irreverence, the denouncing of innocents, and rousing of evil sentiments—no penance can whitewash the responsibility of the sinners nor can any regimen of penitential doings give them a clean bill of acquittal. The pseudosinners look at a lascivious picture and hurry to confession. They yearn for absolution as a key to a peaceful conscience. But the real sinners, those who tear at the very vitals of humanity, they should not be given even the pretense of absolution. Their malevolence raises its ugly head like Hydra and they hurry back from the confessional to more riot and abuse. Kings may go barefoot to Canossa doing penitence, but when they return home, they clutch not the crucifix but the whip. Some of the historic evildoers like Ferdinand and Isabella of Spain each kept their own father confessor; the four of them joined in forming a new Inquisition Incorporated that burned nine thousand Jews and one thousand Moors in one year, the wealthiest of those "pagans," so as to get their fortunes for ships, arms and expeditions.

History is full of penitential despots; what we need is not a world of penitence, but of justice.

PENS

It isn't a man's style that really matters, or his imagination. A writer's worth must be measured by the color of his pen.

Some of the literati swing a blood-red pen and fill the minds of their readers with gore, torture, violence and spilled guts.

Others wield a yellow pen dipped in hate and envy. They love to dye Jews, Gypsies, blacks, reds and sundry others in shades of ugliness, body and soul. The more gall there is in the heart of the writer, the more effective is his pen in brushing half of mankind with a taint of the sinister.

Then again, some writers have a chameleon pen. There is no heart in it and no compassion, no wish for a better world,

139

no care for the suffering. This breed of writer lives by the grace and bribe of the dominant—despot or dictator, king or upstart. They have no color of their own, no direction or leaning. They serve the man in power. At his wink they will say his say and nay his nay, be it on the Volga, on the Yangtze, or the Rhine. They are servants reduced by their own greed, hiding behind the colossus. Their pens stab on command. They are the worst of the lot.

PEOPLE'S DEMOCRACY

People's democracy is a form of government in which the instruments of democracy are locked in a glass case; the people may look at them but never use them. The workers are told they have freedom of thought, of speech, of pen, of assembly, to join a union, to travel, to bear arms—provided they never, *never* remove them from the case. God help the custodian if they ever do!

PETS

We can hardly speak of morals in relation to creatures we systematically devour, mostly singed, but sometimes raw. There are men and women who practice horse love, dog love, cat love. But these very same people take a deer or a calf by its neck, slit its throat, drink the blood, straight or in pudding, and bite off the flesh. And who is to say that a horse they cherish is nobler than a deer they feed on? Indeed, there are nations that eat cats and dogs and others that eat horses but would use a cow only as a work animal.

Some cry over a little goldfish that expired; others travel a thousand miles to catch fish on a nasty hook, for food or mere pleasure.

Some keep frogs to foretell the weather; others cut off their legs and fry them.

Some tenderly husband birds in gilded cages; others serve them for breakfast.

It is all quite confusing. One thought stands out: in a world where man clubs man for gain or sheer gore, there is hardly time to ponder his morals in relation to animals.

PHILOSOPHY

Unlike fish, philosophy does not run in schools. Philosophy is a body of propositions germane to man's relationship to himself and to society. Such theorems bear the stamp of the thinker and need to be examined as to their essential validity. History has no right to endorse a philosopher if he failed to honor fundamental principles of public welfare. The philosophy of a man can be adjudged not by its impressive intricacies but rather by its essential qualities. A philosophy not dedicated to the common good may serve individual evil; it may be no more than an elaborate net of rationalization of certain existing negative facts, a snare in the hands of despots, fanatics, or malevolents.

Philosophy is grounded in ethical principles or it is at best idle, at worst dangerous dialectics. We have seen men like Heidegger or Gobineau prepare metaphysical foundations of virulent race hatred; men like Hegel or Aristotle lend "logic" to Prussian or Macedonian imperialism; men like Fries or Fichte fertilize seeds of anti-Semitism. We have seen great metaphysicians ignore with deliberate coldness outrageous social abuses in their community; raging organized massacres such as the Inquisition, the Crusades, and the full spectrum of judicial and religious savagery went by unnoticed.

I care little for delicate essays on love and God by philosophizing mystics and members of religious orders who fail to arrest hate against heretics and pillage of infidels. I care even less for those among the silent and the nearsighted who lend their names and knowledge in justifying tyranny. Tyranny is villainy and its supporter by silence or by indifference is concerned with little more than his own existence, such as it is. There is need to cut across philosophy with rigorous standards, separating the men who were on the side of the people from

141

those who sided with the people's enemies. Where was Aristotle when his royal pupil Alexander burned Thebes and wantonly left ten thousand Greek women, children and unarmed men in a mound of bloody flesh? Where was the saintly Benedictine when his order burned nine thousand Spanish Jews alive at the stake? Where was Seneca, the tutor of Nero, when droves of innocent captives were driven into Caesar's arena to be devoured by African beasts? Where was Sartre when Stalin turned Russia into one vast prison camp? Where was Heidegger when Hitler garroted, shot or poisoned six million Jews? Where, where hid the so-called great thinkers when the dark princes held scepter?

A philosophy aloof from reality is a chimera; a philosophy in the service of blackguards is sycophantic. Philosophers must be evaluated by what they stood for in times of crisis as well as in times of tranquility. They must be tested by the essence of their contribution to the world's general thrust for freedom.

This world is covered by labels: men, issues, movements, eras, events, religions—they all carry tags. It is the philosopher's task to cast aside the tags and seek out the true reality of existence, the true meaning and the true effect of happenings. The philosopher is forever in search of reality; his is a never ending obligation since this world like all worlds is in perennial flux. *Panta Rei,* as Heraklitos said. Therefore there is no "true" philosophy, but rather *real* philosophy. The philosopher like Diogenes seeks the reality, the ethical as well as logical in all events, past and present. The true philosopher is an incorrigible iconoclast; he may find that sinners have traveled in history as saints and that saints have corrupted the holy man of integrity.

In a world of confusion and corruption, of intellectual abuse and religious intolerance and political perfidy, philosophy must stand like an indestructible bulwark against evil and deceit.

PLIABILITY

Pliability can be brought about by systematic and intense training with the implied threat of expulsion or worse in the background. A Russian or Chinese student, for example, will accept the respective official interpretations in history, sociology, economics, philosophy and other faculties of the liberal arts, or face elimination from the advantageous higher school; if obstreperous, he may, of course, even face punitive action by the authorities.

When you have despotic authorities, there is no objective study or teaching of liberal arts possible. All events and issues in human society are classified by the moguls of the respective dominant political group, be they Lysenko or Stalin or Mao, and their educational security controllers. And if and when the moguls fall, new ones rise into their places and new encyclopedias and texts are prepared for the student masses and teacher masses to accept. The universities and other institutes of higher learning hear no voice of dissent, since in those despotic countries, dissent is tantamount to opposition, which ends invariably in confinement to either an insane asylum, a labor camp, or a prison.

Since this system has prevailed for decades, youth and its teachers have accepted it as the one and only natural form of Marxist society and learned in frustration or indifference to obey the official party line. On rare occasion, martyrs have risen and tried dissent but their number remained few, very few indeed, since the many long ago learned to live by the dictates of the tyrants and not those of their own reason.

POET LAUREATE

Kings used to keep both court poets and court jesters. In "people's democracies" the rulers dislike jests; they carry a tinge of criticism. But the court poets stay on.

143

POLYGAMY

Polygamy is attacked yet practiced in the Occident; in the Orient it is rarely practiced yet widely defended.

POSTERITY

All men are actors of a sort, yet some perform for the day's crowd, others for posterity.

POVERTY

Poverty is a wound on the body politic and can be cured only by treating the whole body.

PRAYER

The Hebrew sages disavowed private prayers; they wanted them liturgistic, that is, public. A man who prays with his people identifies with mankind; a man who prays for himself separates himself from the others. Among the Hebrews, even the individual prayer is of communal character, chanted at specified time and on specified occasion, thereby liturgical.

Personal beseechments of a Divine Being are an expression of either individual desire or individual fear, often in the form of bargaining with the Lord by vows, penance, praise, undue self-denial, extreme humility, sacrifice or other "goods" to tip the scale of divine justice. The pious believer who attempts to change the majestic harmony of Creativity by beseechment is no better than the pagan who places a basket of fruit on the altar or cuts the throat of a goat thereon. Those beseeching God to help them alone on the way to wealth or health want to buy a miracle with words of praise or vows of obedience.

But miracles are immoral in concept. If the Lord can cure one leprous child because of a prayer recited well, why does He leave the others stricken in horrible misery? One who prays for a miracle prays for injustice. Only liturgic suppliants speaking for mankind communicate through their devotions with Divine Justice, and then not for favors but for fairness. Such prayers are profoundly ethical since they praise the Lord as the haven of Love and bow before the altar as the symbol of goodness over greed and generosity over selfishness.

There is no need to flatter the Lord like a vain despot or pile vows before Him like gifts at the feet of an idol—the Lord needs no praise nor does He cherish penance with a purpose behind it. How little they know of the majesty of the Lord who think they can change His eternal course by reciting from the breviary, the missal or the prayer book. All the clicking rosaries, all the prayer wheels turned by hand or by the wind, will not change the mysterious ways of the heavens.

PRECEDENT

The Christian churches of both Rome and Luther burned Jewish books and temples before Hitler did; the churches segregated Jews before Hitler did, and had them wear yellow armbands and yellow spots and funny Jew hats. The churches before Hitler forbade Christians to take service with Jews or to let Jews obtain rights of citizenship. The churches before Hitler forbade any physical or social contact with the God-killers and put Jews by the thousands to the torch, the rack and the sword. The Christian churches only omitted the gas chamber; science had not yet advanced that far.

PRIVILEGES

It is peculiar that those who incessantly criticize the slightest infringement of the privileges of the citizen in democratic countries grant no privileges at all to the inhabitants of their own.

PROGRESS

If man is walking on the two legs of knowledge and humanism, he surely is dragging the latter. Men of this century have tortured, mutilated, blinded and killed more millions of innocent persons than any century before. The Hitler Germans outdid the Huns by a thousand to one; Stalin's Russians made the Mongols look like petty marauders; Mao's market executioners dwarf the misdeeds of Robespierre and the rest of his revolutionary blunderers. India's social reform must still count every seventh citizen as an Untouchable, bound to cloacal and garbage duty for a daily pittance. A Balkan peasant or worker, like his Russian ally, still talks only in his sleep; during the day he is prudently silent. The Arab, on the whole, is under the thumb of one usurping general or another; his feet are bare, his caftan shabby and his body diseased. Communism has given its adherents and satellites an abundance only of poverty.

Perhaps it is time to walk like a man and stop striding with the one leg of science while limping with the other—humanism.

A step forward in the wrong direction is not progress. Nothing is further from the truth than the assumption that replacement of more primitive technical utensils by fancy and complicated gadgets brings society nearer to an improved form of existence.

The replacement of bow and arrow by bazooka or Katusha is not progress.

The replacement of the hot-air balloon by a spying satellite is not progress.

The replacement of a poisoned arrow by poison gas is not progress.

The replacement of battle-trained animals, be they elephants or dogs, by pestilence's germs is not progress.

The replacement of firecrackers by space rockets is not progress.

I could go on and on to show that technical refinement

and know-how do not imply progress in the life of man. Excepting in some medical sectors, achievements in technology and science have more often than not created merely an illusion of progress and nothing more. If we understand by progress a betterment of man's community on earth, we must carefully and objectively examine the effect of each "achievement" upon the coexistence of people and their welfare.

In this year of 1972 we can look back upon a century of immensely publicized "progress." Ours is a century of gadgets and inventions. The array of new scientific and technical toys is dazzling—telephone, telegraph, electric motor, airplane, radio, television, space ships and satellites, electronic utensils galore. Yet in this same century the children of the earth who achieved these toys as the ultimate in progress have butchered by ax or bullet or gas a hundred million people. I will spare the reader further enumeration of mass butcheries in Europe, Africa, Asia and Latin America, all of them done with the help and encouragement if not connivance of the so-called great powers.

I and you, my reader, could have done without all the fancy gadgets and discoveries, had we been spared the massacre of a hundred million innocent people. If progress lies in a better today and a better tomorrow, we have not come closer but rather removed ourselves from it. On my scale a hop to the moon by three pilots does not even the score against a million deaths. And that has been our yearly average: one million murdered by wars and suppression!

I have no appetite for Mars or Jupiter with a million youngsters assassinated on the fields of Asia or Africa, no appetite at all. Why search for rocks afar in space, if the dust right here is daily sprayed with the blood of our young and not so young? I yearn not for the crevasses of the moon; a million innocent unknowns are imprisoned in the jails of Siberia, of China, of Iraq and Czechoslovakia. Keep your space stories and give us back the living bodies of the innocent. That would be progress. The rest is nothing.

PROPAGANDA

The man blinded by propaganda cannot see Truth even if she stares him in the face. Communism is building on the theorem that most people are extremely weak-minded and weak-willed and will in due time accept a most insipid ideology if propagandized long enough. Hitler and his comrade-in-arms Stalin held that the masses will accept even the biggest lie if it is repeated often enough.

The mind is weighted by images and by facts, by personal interests, by fears, by hopes, and finally, by prejudices and old established attitudes. Propagandists about to assail the human mind are fully aware of these conditions underlying the soul of the individual and will proceed in their assigned task accordingly. The propagandists working for a man or group or clique know that the facts can be readily overwhelmed by exaggerated or highly colored images; they can escalate the blurred vision of an accidental mishap into a bloody carnage of deliberate brutality and invest trivia with murderous significance.

All this they can do, and the reverse as well, and thus turn a mountain into an anthill. And before the unaware people have a chance to separate imagery from actuality, fancy and gruesome fiction from fact, they are entangled in the web of propaganda. Propaganda is often to be found in partnership with terror; indeed, terror may take the place of propaganda. In such event terror is the real militating factor while propaganda merely provides the rationale for the terrorized. The regimes of Hitler, Stalin, Mao provide by now classical examples of the Mephistophelian duet.

In despotic society, of which the above trio are most successful protagonists, the members are reduced to utter subservience by the unremitting threat of purges, incarceration, and physical torture. The despot can easily force a victim to grovel before his authority, and confess to the most reprehensible calumny, to save not only his own life, but that of his family. With his confession, the victim himself makes more propaganda on behalf of the despot—a diabolically efficient system!

PROPERTY

The concept of property has been applied not only to physical goods but also and often in history to the rights of man. British, Spanish, Arabic and Portuguese slave traders, who raided black Africa for unpaid servants and workers, sold to the various consumer countries not only the slave's body but also the slave's right to freedom. For the last two enlightened millennia, neither the Christian nor Moslem churches as such endeavored to remove the shame of enslavement for profit from the society of their believers. The same of course applies to the indigent serfs and bonded people in Russia and western Europe.

Ideas and laws propounded in the American, and later, the French Revolution eventually toppled the pyramid of human work abuse—not with the help of the churches and mosques, but rather in spite of them. As institutions, the churches and mosques had little decisive part in abolition even as they had no part in the establishment of civil rights for the black man. In the nineteenth and twentieth centuries, Marxism reiterated in "progressive" form the idea of the government's right to deprive citizens of their freedom, of their property and their work capacity. While Western Europe in the sixteenth, seventeenth and eighteenth centuries robbed fifteen million Africans of their property and all human rights, Communist Russia under Stalin managed to deprive an equal number of its own inhabitants of their belongings and all personal rights by shipping them forcibly, not across the seas, but across the plains of Siberia into work camps. Incidentally, my own father was thus abducted into Siberia, where he spent his declining years in rags in a timber camp, finally dying of exhaustion in 1946. These Siberian "political" slaves were no better off than the Africans in previous centuries who were abducted by European captors to the Americas.

149

While the slaves of the Americas have long been set free, millions of Soviet Russia's "convicted" camp inmates still live on in the horrible work barracks of Siberia. This in no way contradicts the "property" concept of Karl Marx whose communist dictatorship, as represented by a clique of self-perpetuating Central Committeemen or often by one domineering Party Secretary, has the ultimate privilege of depriving so-called capitalists, collaborators, kulaks (landowning small farmers), opportunists, Jews (whom Marx referred to curtly as "usurers" and "international bankers"), deviationists and such, not only of their belongings, but also of all human and civic rights. Indeed, the Siberianized inmates of Russia's labor camps are no less eagerly awaiting their day of liberation than the black slaves of the Americas awaited theirs in the nineteenth century.

PROPORTION

Some faint when a cat gets stepped on; the very same may not blink when a whole city is gassed to death, or even a whole nation.

PROTOCOLS OF ZION

A confused pamphlet of violently anti-Jewish tendency which originated in Czarist Russia and claimed that the Jews were taking over all the continents of the world in a conspiracy directed by the Devil himself from an office in Paris. Listening to late reports coming from Communist Russia, I would say the management of this plot appears to have moved from Paris to Moscow.

PURGE

When Al Capone killed some of his rivals, they called it a massacre; when Stalin massacred hundreds of his lieutenants, they called it a purge! What finesse!

THE QUICK AND THE DEAD

Christians admire only dead Jews, like Jesus, Mary, Joseph, the Apostles, the Evangelists, Paul. Live Jews to them are an annoyance. Live Jews bring out the worst in the Christian. Had the Christians succeeded in killing all the Jews—they almost did—being romantics, they would have written a holy hymn to God's own people, safely dead.

REASON

All men have the power to reason; very few indeed have the will for it. There never was an age of reason, only a spirit of it. What is the breath of reason in the path of the hurricane of gullibility and ignorance?

Reason has little meaning to those whose self-interests dominate their character; to those who have accepted prevalence as a justifiable theory of society; to those who are fearful of disturbing the peace of the established community. It has little meaning to those who submit to religious bias and church ordinance as divine precepts; to those who would rather not investigate the revolting injustices of contemporary moral and legal institutions, the shoddiness of traditionalism; to those whose amiable indifference will direct their activities onto the route of opportunism for personal advantage. The greatest block on the way of reason is self-interest.

Reason's greatest ambition is to prevail.

REBELS

Youth has a right to rebel, which means "to make war again." But that war must be against the enemies of mankind, not its friends. Unfortunately despotism in its darkest form has fastened its grip on many of the youth groups and by cunning propaganda is misleading them to fight not the forces of communist suppression, but those of democratic decency. So-called Marxists, Maoists and Soviet Kremlinists have managed by years of brainwash to confuse or bribe youth leaders turning them against the truly humanitarian among their elders and even to persuade the rebellious that by burning homes, hospitals, and shops they will hasten an alleged revolution. The very same Red oligarchs, by incessantly repeating the Big Lie, and the Big Smear of humanity's truly great leaders, created in the young a naive ideology according to which revolution will come about if one bombs a bank toilet, derails a suburban train or throws dynamite into a college dorm.

In all this, the "leftists," as they like to call themselves, are no more than moronic pawns, black or white, in the shifty hands of the Communist establishment—an establishment that commands by sheer terror absolute subservience of its citizenry to its Red bosses who possess all the splendors that Stalinist-type society offers to its party head and his entourage, from Peking Palace to fleets of Rolls Royce cars, women in Parisian boudoirs, lakeside dachas with private gardeners, and so on. The private parties thrown by the Red bigwigs from Budapest to Moscow, from Belgrade to Peking, differ little from the festivities ordered by the Oil Kings of Arabia.

It would be comical, were it not so tragic, to see a million western college students who live in affluence and total freedom genuflect before the pictures of those Communist oppressors whose citizens sweat on the primitive "people's farms" of Russia or China, clothed in shabby rags, men with only one pair of breeches as their property, lacking most of the little possessions of the western peoples, lacking even such minimal requirements as toilet paper or private bathrooms.

This is the tragicomedy of present-day youth movements. They worship a make-believe Red society in which citizens in actuality can enjoy neither freedom of speech, freedom of assembly, freedom of the pen, freedom of travel, freedom to vote by secret ballot, nor freedom, of anything! Among those miserable, frightened serfs of Russia and China, where millions have been kept for decades in labor camps and prisons— those who were not decapitated in public marketplaces of Canton or shot in the back of the head in Lubjanka Prison— among those poor victims of Communist reversion to Red feudalism, scores of our "left" youth see a chimeric panorama of progressive tranquility!

REFORMERS

Some plainspoken folk are honestly out to change the world; some flamboyant reformers are just out to make a quick dollar.

The great reformers were not all for humanity, but then again, not all for themselves. And they never lost the dream of a better tomorrow.

REINCARNATION

Reincarnation is the Hindu form of immortality. The dead live on after death, not in an angelic heaven or the Islamic type of paradise, but right here on earth, in a natural shape and manner, be it as a prince or a pauper or even a beetle. Some Hindus wear bells on their toes to scare away ants and the like, so as not to accidentally kill their own departed cousins. Even as some Christians (very few, indeed) avoid pitfalls of sin that lead to hell, and some Moslems perform honeyed acts to, in the windup, reach paradise with its delectable dishes and devastating houris, so do Hindu ritualists on occasion do the proper act instead of the self-gratifying one, just on the hunch that they might otherwise, post mortem, find themselves embodied in a snake or spider.

The Hebrews have no tradition of a personal heaven, only a strong faith that the soul dies not with the body.

RELIGION

Religion in spite of its noble prophets has a melancholy record. There was a time when mankind was bereft of true faith and rife with primitive paganism, superstition and sanguine ritual. We now have three billion adherents to the great religions—and kill more people in one year than the "savages" did in a century.

RENEGADES

Those who attack their own will easily find an audience among others.

RETIREMENT

You retire a horse, not a man. The horse at least can graze; man must work or disintegrate.

Life is a great feast; let us not exclude those from the table who no longer dine noisily, full of silly argument and gossip. Let us find places of dignity for them at the feast of life without patronizing the older members.

Let us remember, in the eyes of Mother Nature a century is but a blink of the lashes. Youth is very brief indeed; and age always awaits.

REVERENCE

Some great scoundrels bear revered names. It is time to unmask the rogues and killers who stalk through the pages of history, adorned in laurels and lily-white togas by ancient sycophants.

REVOLUTIONARIES?

They fill the campus arenas, the street corners, the court-house steps. They shout obscenities, they insult the author-ities, they attack the establishment. They are a holy fury. Who? The great bands of "revolutionaries" in the safe de-mocracies! They yell slogans against dictatorship!—not in Russia or China where dictatorship exists, but in the United States where such yelling is permitted. They yell in four-letter words at fascism, not in Portugal or Brazil where it exists but in the United States where you can call your elected president a dirty fascist and no one will imprison you.

We have a plague of those pestiferous revolutionaries

who besmirch this great democracy with such terms as fascist, tyrannical, oppressive, piggish, police state, and so on. These very same "radicals" can be seen abroad in the truly despotic countries walking about quietly like mice, not daring to raise their voices. I would like to see the visiting American students in the communist countries, and there are many thousands of such students, raise their voices against despotism in Russia, or in any of the other tyrannical states.

REWARD

If you thank the Lord for your bounty, you have to berate Him for poverty, evil and sickness. He needs neither praise like a Caesar nor curses; be yourself and on your own, but do the will of God, the will of Goodness.

God is not a crutch for the weak or a plume for the powerful. Work for the Good and fight for Justice and you are on His side. God will not pay you off if you do right; righteousness is its own reward. God will not place you in a special paradise if your heart stands fast against evil. Your courage carries with it its own satisfaction. Be reckless if evil is about; withstand it with all your power. Your victory, the victory of goodness, is all you will receive.

Don't be a mercenary of God; His soldiers are free men and fight not for booty. In ordinary armies, there are ranks and medals and fanfare and fancy uniforms; among the Lord's troops all this is meaningless. Popes have sinned, and bishops, by failing to heed God's inner call to all true believers: Justice to *all* children below the heavens. God is not in cathedrals and stands not before your altars. God cannot hear your prayers or your praises of the Lord. But He hears the voices of the hungry, the cry of children in anguish, the weeping of battle widows and the groans of those tortured by oppressors.

Save your prayers and supplications; God is pleased by neither. He is deaf to self-seeking reward hunters or those overwhelmed by their own luck. Don't praise the Lord as if

He were Caesar or kneel before Him as if He were Attila. Stand up before God and keep your hands and heart at the task for Justice and Freedom. And before all, be good to fellow man: the love of God to man and the love of man to man are of the same divine flame which the Hebrews called *Shekinah*.

RITUALISM

There is a strong tendency in our time to brush aside religious rituals and deride cults. Essentially, cults were only the bottle from which the wine of belief was poured to the willing and not so willing. After a while, more often than not the wine had gone or spoiled, but the bottles remained. Many observances of religious rituals are today dried up and meaningless; many of the precepts are doubtful. The Talmudists divide the ritualistic precepts into two kinds, the Explainable ones *(Dinim)* and the Inexplicable *(Chukim)*.

We of course no longer accept the holiness of the cow as the Hindus did and still do, or the holiness of the Egyptian's cat or the bear of the Ainus. But quite a few of the religious rituals are still widely prevalent. The issue in ethics is only whether they are taken as fruitful symbolic observances, as reminders of benevolent activity towards fellow man today, or are accepted superstitiously and formalistically as acts in themselves by the mere performance of the ritual to have fulfilled their religious duties. The student of ethics must regard the ritualist as socially negativistic if he or she carries out the symbolic acts as reality—a spurious reality indeed! If, on the other hand, the ritualist deals out the amulets as allegoric reminders of the essentially needful, then they can be constructive in shaping a truly better community.

You cannot take holy communion, drink the blood and eat the flesh of Christ and think yourself a Christian. You must act out and persistently do deeds of fairness, goodness and tolerance to *all*—regardless of prejudice, racial, religious or snobbish—to become a Christian. Christ takes on the sins of man only if man takes on the Logos of Christ. The Logos of Christ is goodness to every man, tolerance and fairness. It is no cross to bear to be a Christian; goodness is not so heavy, tolerance is not so onerous a burden, and fairness no millstone around the neck.

Christ just on the lips is no Christ at all. By their deeds thou shalt recognize the great multitudes of "Christians" as pagans. If Christ is their faith, they are disbelievers. There is enough goodness in the Gospels to give everyone a good life; enough goodness in the Koran to make this world a place of solace; a strength of kindness in the Old Testament to override all human hate on this earth. But merely miming the cults of these or other religions solves nothing and confuses everything.

ROMANCE

Romance is expectancy, curiosity, wonderment. If those three are gone, have failed to appear, there is nothing to the great dramas of life. Without those three, there is no love, only sex; no adventure, only experience; no dialogue, only conversation. What a loss for the many who have never felt the touch of these three!

For some, the three graces appear only in their youth and for a golden decade they partake of the dream life in love, dedication and adventure. How thrice blessed the soul that never grows old, hardened or blasé!

SACRIFICE

There are so many who are ready to die for an idea, a Utopia, the defense of their homeland or their ruler, or just a dare, a prize, a bet. Where are those who are willing to *live* for an idea, a Utopia, their homeland? To live for something, something better, something truly great—not just exist, but live for the better world of tomorrow?

SAINTS

Saints have not pushed the world ahead; sinners have. Saints have escaped the world; sinners wouldn't want to.

SATAN

Many who reached out to touch God found themselves holding hands with the devil. The Germans genuflected before the Teutonic power and there was Hitler; the Russians worshiped the Little Father, and there was Stalin; the Chinese made obeisance to Confucius, and out sprang Mao! Perhaps God has walked out on us and we are left confronting Satan.

SAVAGES

Savages: a term applied in earlier centuries to men of the woods, remote from the refinements of civilization, specifically to American Indians. The fate of America's Indians is well known to students of the last five centuries. But as these lines are written, hundreds of thousands of savages or jungle people of Brazil, Guatemala and other Latin American territories are being liquidated in the most beastly manner.

Military expeditions are sent out by ruthless authorities in Brazil, for instance, to push back the savages and thus obtain lands for certain influential industrial circles.

But, then again, why should the "discoverers" of today differ from those of previous centuries? Columbus, Cortez, Pizarro and the rest came for gold and gems. Even the Church was used by the conquerors of old to lend a measure of legitimacy to the blatant thieves' carnival. Who were the savages then? Who are the savages now? Certainly not the people of the forest and the mountains! The whole world accepted the new word genocide in condemnation of its horridness. Shall this agreement remain a mere achievement of semantics? Where are the churches built in the name of the saintly Hebrew Jesus? Do their quarrels over celibacy, birth control and the powers of bishops leave them no time to concern themselves with the cruel massacre of the forest people of the Americas?

SCIENCE

Science is an angel carrying two torches, one to bring light to this dark earth, the other to burn vegetation, homes and people.

SCUM

Scum floats to the top.

SELECTIVITY

It is amazing to observe those tender souls whose empathy throbs for convicted police-killers remain totally indifferent to the death of a million besieged Biafran women and children or a million Bengalis. What discriminating creatures those empathizers be!

160

SELF-PRESERVATION

Self-preservation is acceptable as the one and only driving motive in animal life; it does not suffice as validation of human deeds. Man raised in free society must be thought to value the voice of conscience. In despotic society conscience is replaced by servility and ingrained obedience to despotic programs. In free society man is instructed to abhor murder and cruelty; in the despotic society of fascism or communism, human conscience is adjudged a weakness, an evil weakness to be cast aside for the sake of "the Cause."

SERENITY

The world may appear on many a day quiet as a bayside in the shade—yet in those still waters a million creatures, tiny and turbulent, are engaged in incessant and vicious struggle for mere existence.

SERMONS

Sermons by clergymen except on rare occasions and simple basic subjects should be eliminated. Instead let the minister or priest or rabbi read from the great literature of his tradition. I find it unimpressive to have a young, or even older, graduate of a theological seminary lecture a contemporary audience in New York, Paris or London on a recent book and its author, his knowledge being obviously quite limited, while there are a score of professionals or semiprofessionals of that field sitting in the pews. I find it overbearing to have these same preachers offer profound statements on current plans and projects of the heads of the government while elected representatives sit in the audience listening with bored expressions or signs of obvious annoyance.

Preachers are ordained to advise and counsel on matters of morals and interpretation of *materia theologica*. Beyond the borders of religion, the competence of the minister is rather questionable. In addition, preachers are often obliged to deliver from two to four sermons a week to different groups on diverse topics. This procedure, which I find highly objectionable, reduces the rhetoric of the professional clergyman to unavoidable superficiality. Taking into account all available handbooks for the minister, he still finds before him the insurmountable task of giving a serious and documented lecture on a current topic almost extemporaneously before a public which in Western European urban society is to a considerable extent his equal, and often his better.

It is time, high time, to free the minister from these onerous lecture tasks. And let him confine himself to the Bible and religious tradition. Let the journalists, the politicians and the after-dinner lecturers discuss the latest novel, current events, space travel and the paradoxical utterances of the governmental administration.

SERVILITY

There is a trace of the servant in every man, a willingness to render absolute obedience to the powers that be in return for one's safety and sustenance: The young man who is eager in times of tranquility to submit to military discipline for meager pay, throwing all worry to the wind; the man who prefers the status of a gentleman's man, avoiding tha of an independent man with all the direct responsibilities i. entails. Yes, these are familiar examples of the little person who daydreams of security through some higher-up and enters service with a devotional expression in his or her eyes.

Yet that same servility is not hidden by the fancy uniforms of many a ranking official in dictatorial establishments in the oppressive lands from Russia to China, from Albania to Algiers. Those who solicit the rewards of high employment from the ruling group by implication also undertake to carry out all the wishes of their masters. We thus hear an eminent Russian physicist applaud the rape of a small neighboring country as a blessing for the victim and deride the charity of democratic lands as a malevolent deed. This scholar, like so many others in his circumstances, has let the servant in him grow to mastery over his chameleon soul. These achievers in totalitarian countries have traded their consciences for gratuities. Their golden medals proclaim them Heroes of Soviet Servility.

SEXUAL HEALTH

Sex is of little import for those who have it in vigor. It becomes a magnified issue where weakness underlies.

There has been a great intensification of "sexual permissiveness" and "sex education" over the last ten years. I see little rise in sex health because of this alleged candor, but a depressing rise in venereal disease.

SHORTCUT

Take a shortcut and you may miss the most beautiful vistas.

SILENCE

Silence can be and often is, in history, of all crimes the most devious and reprehensible. It is caused by man's most deplorable determination to keep his own ship running before the wind regardless of who and how many perish in the sea through his unwillingness to stand by.

Silence is a crime when speaking up could help the victim. The sin of omission is often as great as that of commission. Especially, the man who by wearing the cloth has assumed the burden of being in the Lord's service has lost all grace if he hides behind the curtain of anonymity and rests his tongue. The clergy spends too much time in the vestry and not enough in the street. It is no arduous task to move your lips in prayer before a head-bent flock locked in pews;

but the people in the pews go out into the streets and that is where they live and hate and kill. It is there that the clergyman is needed.

Where is the clergy when the barricades are up? Where is the clergy when the dogs are set upon children? Where is the clergy when club and hose and shot are used against a suppressed minority? Maybe they are kneeling in prayer at the altar? Maybe they are reading the Good Book? No book is good when it keeps a man from freedom's struggle and no prayer is worth saying that keeps a man from cursing the devil, to his face and loudly.

Silence is the devil's tongue when the world cries out for a protest.

SIN

The trouble with the adherents of Christianity is that they are looking for sin in themselves instead of outside themselves. While they are clearing out the harmless moths harbored in their souls, the true enemies of peace on earth, the villainous self-seekers and oppressors, go about their ugly business almost unimpeded. While Hitler was drawing a bloody curtain over Europe, the German Christians were running to weekly confessions, whispering to tired priests admissions of guilt to having eaten wurst on Friday or, worse yet, having had sex illegitimately.

The Christians, Protestants and Catholics alike, are hunting for the devil in themselves while deviltry conquers the world. Christianity has filled up its followers with guilt feelings and self-criticism instead of teaching them to abhor the oppression of free peoples and ambitious aggressors.

It is amazing with what intensity of feeling Christian clergymen express their pleas to God to forgive their sins, which I am sure were minute infractions of traditional prohibitions! Yet millions of innocent women and children and unarmed civilians are butchered before their eyes, without the holocaust seeming evidence of sin. It appears that some silly flicker of sex in them or their flocks troubles the clergymen so much that they lose sight of those who sin with ax and machine gun.

Primitive man asked forgiveness of his god by buying him off with a sacrifice of grain or cattle. God, being a despot, had to be propitiated by offerings. Man accepts by and large a roster of sins determined by his respective religious denomination and when he feels himself transgressing, he is ready to confess and obtain forgiveness by penance. Man rarely questions the merit of the Code of Sins, much of which is no more than venerable church discipline without any intrinsic moral value.

Blasphemy is not a sin, but a state of mind; self-abuse is not a sin, but lack of mental hygiene; fornication is not a sin but a style of life; homosexuality is not a sin but a sickness; heresy is not a sin but a parting of ways; vanity is not a sin, but lack of insight. I could go on and list a great number of paragraphs in the Code of Sin that need expunging but then there would be very little of this troublesome piece of ecclesiastic jurisprudence left for the priests to enforce and perhaps they would have to put away entirely their manuals of penance.

Sin occurs if you hurt your fellow man; nothing else is sinful, though it may be foolish or feeble. But if you are of malevolent character, your sins cannot be forgiven and no bag of penitent prayers or contrite vows can absolve the blood of Cain. Thinking men understand the role of evildoers in the chain of criminal events. They want rioters and political cannibals not on the torture rack, but in front of free jurors, instead of in the governmental mansion.

SLAVERY

Essentially, institutional religion in all its denominations has neither thwarted nor opposed the institution of slavery. Christianity, Islam, Hinduism and so on have accepted slavery as part of what their proponents all considered civilized society. To the religious inhabitants of ancient Hellas, all foreigners were barbarians and destined to be slaves. The Hebrews failed to abolish slavery, [although they set a limit to the time of servitude permissible] yet they themselves were the victims of bondage. Peoples as far apart as the Sumerians, Carthaginians and Incas did not reject the social abuse implicit in a slave society. Renowned philosophers of the past like Aristotle, Augustinus and Thomas Aquinas supported the separation of persons into free and bound not only as just, but as divinely ordained.

In our time, the National Socialist Germans reduced their Jewish and Gypsy citizens and neighbors to slave status, depriving them even of the right to live. Stalin's Soviet Russia and Mao's China have reduced millions of their citizens to total rightlessness, which has been fully reported by former sufferers of such deprivations. Indeed the villeins of England, the *hörige* of Germany, the serfs of Czarist Russia bring us to the last century. Still, the treatment of slaves by kings and czars was probably better than that of the commissars of the communist empires, let alone the German concentration camp führers. In all these centuries from the days of the pharaohs to the present time of Communist imperialism, the churches as institutions have had a tolerant eye for the utmost abuse of human body and mind by ruling cliques.

SOCIOLOGY

Sociology or the study of society began over a century ago as a serious endeavor and dropped over the decades into a melee of a hundred faces, some sad, more concerned, some bewildered and more just clowning. When you hear Soviet sociologists at international conventions attack American sociological practices as reactionary while in their own Marxist provinces the slightest whisper of discord results in the confining of the citizen to an insane asylum or a Siberian labor camp—well, they see the splinter but not the beam.

There is no serious sociology possible under a despotic

166

regime, be it fascist or communist. The criticism of Russian sociology by Mao's China is twice removed from honesty. Fear ends all objectivity and reason in the chains of terror will bespeak its anguish, not its truth.

SOVIET RUSSIA

What bothers me is not Russia's scarcity of private cars but the paucity of passports for her citizens to travel abroad. America has twenty million passports to Russia's two hundred thousand. The poor termite in the tunnel thinks that's all there is to the world.

Soviet Russia grants its citizens four little freedoms: the freedom to be silent, the freedom not to see, the freedom not to hear, and the freedom to say yes!

SPACE FICTION

We are offered astrological predictions, scientifically arrived at with the aid of computers. We have seen science in the service of militarism, despotism, fanaticism (Hitler's technological torture and execution chambers). We now see science as a handmaiden of superstition. We also encounter science as a wheel for spinning space fairy tales. Writers attuned to the curious and gullible spin stories of space monsters, gassy, liquid, limpid and otherwise. Midgety wonder creatures of the galaxies growing feelers like a snail, three-eyed and four-legged, giants of King Kong size breathing paralyzing breath from green nostrils are finally tamed by space hostesses in miniskirts or captains in cadet uniforms constantly fingering the buttons of computers.

Science has opened great vistas for the space hacks who fill the avenues of communication with shrewdly invented planetary peoples, transported hither in their saucer-like vehicles. When the scientists hesitated, having nothing to report beyond a dull chapter on stone and gasses with a mere hint of common minerals, the space hacks looked up and announced: "Man is not alone. Billions of rare creatures populate the up-there universe!" I venture to say that more adults have become addicted to reading space fairy tales than juveniles; after all, it is "scientific." Some of the determined writers have even come out with affidavits "proving" that they had conversations with saucer people—in good American of course—and scores of innocents of that race that never dies out have sworn to the verity of their hallucinations.

But then again, if the Hindus and Greeks could dream of men in the moon and demigods on the sun, why can't space devotees do it today?

Space prophets who hectically bang away at stories of space people on strange planets, and the like, remind me of the evangelical scribes expanding on the pleasures of heaven and the horrors of hell. The masses quite often accept pure bunk as authentic if presented by holy professionals.

SPACE SCIENCE

As long as the nations on earth live in constant wars of mutual destruction, cold wars, hot wars, gas wars, class wars, genocide and fratricide—at the moment, the count is nine separate bloody contests with others coming up—as long as the earthlings cannot civilly manage their own lands, it is immoral, even foolish for them to attempt acquisition of properties on other planets.

The endeavor of some of our nations, competitive of course, to probe closely distant planets and galaxies in search of minute data on geology is wanton and paradoxical. We have, God knows, little enough space assigned to us here on this mossy rock we call World—yet every inch of its soil is soaked with human blood spilled in vile competitive battles. Why these ridiculous efforts to add to our territory if we are totally unable or unwilling to live man next to man, in peace and harmony? Our leaders, enough of them to keep us steadily on the warpath, our savage seekers of power are ridden by unbridled ambition for property, dominance and lust, and the wide mass of people are either unable or unwilling to depose the vipers.

Why the tragicomedy of space search? We would as certainly bloody up the moon and Jupiter and Mars and Venus as we have spilled the blood of our neighbors into our riverbeds and on our meadows. Man has no right to pretend to a search for faraway lands if his own have since time immemorial been no more than battlegrounds. And if we have no power or mind to overthrow earth's false ideologies and trivial religions, why pretend to bring light to faraway while all is black and bitter nearby?

Perhaps some coming millennium will have the right to carry the torch to space; we have not. Let's forget the planets. We got rocks from the moon; we have nothing to offer in return to the world of space but our wars and our miseries.

Now that we have a basketful of lunar rocks, perhaps we can go back to use the big money for housing and feeding the poor and care of the aged. We still live in a world where the majority of its inhabitants lead a life closer to that of an ancient cliff dweller than that of a western burgher.

We got from the moon a barrel of rocks, the possession of which is of little significance. Of the world's hundred and fifty nations, only six made an effort even to examine them. One thing the moon trip proved for sure is that whatever we learned, we knew beforehand, and that we could have acquired such information without a personal inspection by half a dozen pilots.

Hack science writers for the last ten years filled up our libraries and journals with fantastic outpourings. They have used and abused the gullible public and filled them with expectation of things to come, floating in space ships. This is no better than witchcraft tales in the Middle Ages. The young and the very young, especially, have been pitilessly exploited by the hucksters of space science. Hard scientific facts were hardly able to stop this avalanche of space nonsense. Nothing inhabits those planets but the money-bent imagination of the literary hucksters and it is high time to cleanse our youth and

169

those who never grew up of the nuisance of space superstitions.

Our billion cliff dwellers are waiting, anxiously waiting, hungrily waiting for the bread and house and health that our limited funds can give them. Let's shoo the space hucksters away from the funds and turn them over to the really concerned for the advantage of the billion cliff dwellers who cry out for a share in our world. Let us reach out for the poor, the old and the sick on earth, not humor the ambitions of the moonstruck.

SPERM

You can breed calves today with the frozen sperm of a long-dead bull. Can one improve the human race by such genetic methods—sperm banks for the betterment of mankind? To begin with, great scientists, great artists, great philosophers come overwhelmingly from average stock; and in turn, great achievers as well as outstanding talents sire as a rule average descendants. I doubt if any eager geneticist could change these patterns for the better.

And what is "better"? The world is full of erudite people, gifted artists and cunning scientists. More of them will not make this a finer world. Germany's foremost dramatist, Gerhart Hauptmann, joined voluntarily and proudly Hitler's councils as did Germany's foremost philosopher, Martin Heidegger, and foremost composer Richard Strauss. Russia's honored scientists still ornament the Communist dictator's hardbitten antidemocratic propaganda machine. Knowledge, art, and technology make its representatives not better, only more dangerous. Russia's top spaceman and woman are in the forefront of their political despot's propaganda machine against all, but all, principles of civic liberties and personal rights of the western world. And in Red China the individual scientist or scholar emphasizes no less than the prize-winning factory worker that he owes it all to the *Quotations* of Chairman Mao. We have an ample supply of accomplished men in our

170

midst; what we need is not more achievers, but more men of good will. What good is a world of hybrid intellects and literati if it is under the thumb of a cold-blooded dictator whose every ugly whim they obey in greedily nurturing their careers? Our need is for ethical leaders on the top and honestly good people in the rank and file. Our desperate need is for kindness of man to man, not an increased accumulation of conniving achievers. Science as readily serves the dictatorial monster as the gentle head of a true republic. I have heard a host of technologists, scientists and performers take the American republic to task; I have scarcely heard one of them, from Kapitza on down, direct a single critical remark toward the Kremlin clique. The silence of the achievers in Soviet Russia is not golden, only yellow.

STATUES

Why are so many statues of outstanding men on horseback? Is the horse a symbol of wisdom or devotion? And why are there so few statues of women?

STATUS

All men strive for status, some for momentary prestige in social life, others for a lasting image in posterity's eyes.

SUICIDE

Suicide, or the endeavor to make an end to an unbearable life was, and still is, regarded in England as a felony. The origin of such jurisprudence lies in the rigid interpretation of law by despotic governments. The subject living in the domain is the possession of the respective ruler and by doing away with himself, he destroys his owner's property. The religions of the East have a more enlightened attitude towards the suicide. In the Shinto hara-kiri or later kamikaze, the Vedic suttee, the traditional Hebraic self-destruction in the face of overwhelming enemies, examples are found of suicide as an attempt at positive, individualist decision to choose death in place of a dishonorable or empty life. In a way, Golgotha and Socrates' taking hemlock are symbols of suicide; Jesus and Socrates could have escaped death but they held their causes immeasurably higher than personal suffering and personal extinction. The soldier throwing himself on the bursting bomb, the father jumping in front of the lance aimed at his son, the hero covering the retreat of his comrades with his own body, the accused taking poison to avoid betraying his family or friends under threatening torture—are they to be classified as criminals, as many western countries still do?

A man has the right to commit homicide in self-defense and a man has the right to commit suicide in defense of a cause or issue greater than himself. The Buddhist monk who sets his frail body on fire to inflame the spirit of freedom in his countrymen is heavens above the moralizing church organization that inveighs against suicide at the altar of his oppressors.

SUPERSTITIONS

People ridicule superstitions of others while cherishing their own.

TAKING SIDES

Taking somebody's side is not enough; make sure you take his good side.

TEACHING

Germans produced Hitlerism and Russians Stalinism not so much because of what they were teaching, but rather because of what they failed to teach.

We have had teachers for the crown's sake, teachers for God's sake, teachers for business' sake, teachers for science's sake but none yet for man's sake. It is less than two hundred years since man became free with the American and French revolutions. Until then, nine out of ten persons lived as serfs or hirelings at the command and whim of their respective despotic rulers. And many of the ugliest traditions of the pre-Enlightenment era still claim the minds or bodies of people in various parts of the world. Even in our own freest of nations, there are dark corners of suppressive race prejudices and legalistic barriers keeping an unfortunate minority of citizens from the unencumbered pursuit of happiness.

The youth go to schools on all levels of education, giving time and attention to sundry subjects, serious and frilly as well, but the subject of *ethics* is anathema; it is left to the discretion of parents who inherited their prejudices from generations of slavers or other bigots unwashed by social progress. There seems to be time left in all our schools for sports and recreation, but none for the study of ethics. The few universities offering courses in morals do so in detached manner as part of philosophical history or as a pathology of human be-

173

havior. But ethics are not to be surveyed quizzically by dull anthropologists or bored philosophy instructors.

Ethics are an essential theme of education, an integral part of pedagogy, indeed, the heart of training a child to be a free and understanding person. Unless a student is given an ethical regulative, he or she has no means of judging right from wrong, positive from negative. All the voluminous information placed in the mind of the child remains shelf-wisdom, unadjusted, meaningless. What good is the knowledge of the seven seas and all the thousand ports, if the ship carries no compass?

The students in Alabama, for example, learn of anthropology, philosophy, sociology, history, law and religion, but they toss on the sea of knowledge no better directed than a villein in the feudal era, because they have never been taught in school the principles of ethics. Their parents and grandparents at home raised them in the lowest tradition of white supremacy. They think themselves entitled to an overbearing, exclusive preference because their skin is beige and some of their neighbors are ebony. A state or country that is only a few decades away from keeping humans like cattle in slave stables has no right to leave the teaching of ethics to the parents descended from slave drivers, who in their arrogance wish to retain the double standard of the old social structure. It is, rather, imperative that classes in ethics be conducted, activistic, profoundly directed study courses by instructors of high standards who would impress upon the minds of the students the folly and immorality of the traditional conduct of their ancestors and imbue them with the spirit and text of life in a free and truly democratic society. Instead of leaving their uninformed minds to marinate in domestic prejudice, school would send students home with the message and demands of a new era.

We have seen that the tender hearted, who asked for "gradual" elimination of racial evils, have accomplished nothing in a hundred years of alleged equality under the Constitution. It is touching how concerned they are with the sensitivities of loud-mouthed racists—yet how indifferent to the sensitivities of the victims! The same of course applies to the teaching of the youth in South Africa with its own "colored" and black problem, India with its Untouchables, in fact to all the countries in both hemispheres.

Mankind can get along with less business, less religion, even less science, but it will never live in harmony without ethics. What good is improvement in comfort offered by business, purification of ritualism urged by religion, or acceleration in speed rushed by science, if right here in the very back yard of humanity, man carries on like a savage? Without the teaching and the subsequent victory of ethics in a free and equitable society, business will serve in the main a privileged class; religion, while offering loud homilies on the sufferings of the saints, will keep silent about lynchings at the church gate; and science will remain engrossed by the military while laying a small tithe on the altar of public welfare.

TELEOLOGY

There is as little purpose in nature as in a rock rolling down a hill. Nature is set up so that creature must devour creature, with all the terror such a bestial process involves! A hen may have its legs eaten one after another while still alive and watching her killer fox; a fish is eaten up piece by piece by a larger fish; an anguished frog is swallowed by a gulping snake, and so on.

Nature is massacre, stealth, unabated, intermingled with minor and major catastrophes that help add to the horror of senseless death and destruction.

There is no fine plan in nature—just disorder, breeding, and killing. Nothing gets better, nor is there a progress by higher life or order in the making. If you walk a Sudanese valley a million years old or search in deep waters older than that, all you find is traces of the same meaninglessness of greedy eaters and terrified, unsuccessful, would-be escapees. The crocodile of a hundred million years ago devoured the river animals then even as the one of today rips them apart now. The handsome bluebird of aeons ago still picks off waterflies and crickets and May flies as deftly as ever, only to be beaten down by hawkish wings and talons. Such is the structure of nature, no sense, no progress, no purpose, no secret underlying plan except fulfillment of life's most primitive, most all-pervading motto: shark eats shark and the worms eat all.

The theologies and teleologies are made by man, frightened man, who vainly tries to overcome his fears by wishing into reality a refined purpose of progress, or a second life so much better than the one down here, the horror of which cannot escape him. What a divine dream! But dreams are only for the sleeper, the deep sleeper!

TERMINOLOGISM

Terminologism is the art of camouflaging a mediocre mind behind a screen of new words or old words assigned a new meaning. When you look closely at the new word creations, good old banality shows underneath the trivia.

Some philosophers imagine that if they create a new word, or attribute to an old word a meaning different from what is currently accepted, they have got a new idea, a metaphysical homunculus. In fact, they only impose upon the reader a need to prepare for himself a glossary of their newly coined words, since without such the reader would be at a loss to understand them. Among the modern philosophers, Immanuel Kant, Edmund Husserl, and Martin Heidegger (the sage of the Third Reich) are the classical examples of this narcissistic attitude. When you are all through assembling their respective glossaries, you discover that fundamentally you have learned nothing except new words for old verities or old platitudes. The heart of the matter remains as mysterious to you as before you read these particular works; you have merely added to your body of knowledge groups of *termini-technici* favored by these men.

176

The writings of the philosophical terminologists seem to have a great attraction to many interested in metaphysical problems, since man is more often than not more attracted by half-truths and cloudy symbols than by plain thought and plain talk. Thus the lofty word-snobbism leads naturally to inverted discussions and dissertations which add burden to the already much overloaded chariot of philosophy. My personal opinion is that the philosopher who cannot use our own existing language can hardly be expected to add to our understanding by a synthetically fabricated form of expression.

During the last fifty years in the field of logic a number of mathematicians and linguists were engaged in trying to reduce our standard manner of writing and speaking into a form of philosophical shorthand or mathematical symbolism, which of course was intended to simplify matters. All this means is that people interested in philosophy should take a year's course in the meaning of the meaning of this type of mental play. When they are all through and thoroughly comprehend the different types of shorthand of the pseudo-mathematicians and semanticists, when they reach the very peak of logical positivism, they know no more and no less than when they began. No one has ever improved understanding of matter or mind by mere terminological affectations.

THOUGHT

He lives twice who lives and thinks. But a thought that does not move you to active participation is no more than idle conversation with yourself.

TITLES

Titles are the currency of sycophants. Despots throughout history, having usurped for themselves the top seat at the table, then dish out titled places to their subservients. It is amazing how even highly civilized people become so imbued with tradition that they behold this most dishonorable procedure of bestowing honorifics on obeisant subjects with awe and envy. Of course, the loudest paper buntings are placed by the palace dwellers upon their own headpieces. Emperors of China, kings of France and Comrade Stalin had court grovelers refer to them as Son of Heaven, King, or Father of the Nation. Kings and queens of Spain and England flattered themselves with epithets like Defender of the Faith, Emperor of India and the Dominions Beyond the Seas, by the Grace of God, and so on and on. Among the latter-day dictators, Trujillo strutted about with a nimbus of The Benefactor and Illustrious Superiority; Nkrumah was hailed as Osagyefo (Redeemer); the king of Siam topped them all with his title as the Super-Almighty. Some of the most arrogant rulers dealing out titles and medals to their kowtowing entourage considered themselves omnipotent in four or five letters: *Duce* Mussolini and *Führer* Hitler.

The English bask in the tepid waters of a bygone offensive aristocracy. One now a bank clerk inherits the title of earl, which implies ownership of a county; indeed, his wife is referred to as countess. Storekeepers are granted the title of knight, which in feudal times meant a great nobleman's military attendant. On the other hand, a baron inherits the title and the designation Lord because one of his ancestors was privileged to serve the king as a chief tenant over villeins and serfs. Above them all rank the dukes, inheriting their titles and lands from hereditary minor despots within the realm. Royal dukes are also entitled to crown subsidies.

One might argue that these titles are without serious implication, serfdom having been abolished, and the once absolute authority of dukes and such obliterated. If this be the case, then it is time to abolish the sham of titleage, royal and otherwise, whereby distinctions are created within the people by alleged rulers who are in fact only dupes or fronts.

It is immoral to accept persons as being of high social status because one of their ancestors was a queen's lover or a queen's pirate, a king's henchman or a king's trusty master over miserable serfs. There is a stench to these royal privileges, the stench of dungeon, double-dealing, bondage, poverty and misery. It is a cheap way for despots to reward their gang, be they barons or *gauleiters*. In a free and ethical society, no man stands above his fellow citizens, neither by so-called noble birth nor the grace of a dictator. In a free and ethical society, men stand alongside each other—none above, none below.

TOMBSTONES

Our sages say that when the soul of a deceased is not held down by a sanctified tombstone on a grave, that soul will wander to the four corners of the world and weep and wail against such heathen abuse. And so it is, that six million souls of Jews and Jewesses, infants and senescents alike, peregrinate in twilight and darkness, having no consecrated ground to rest in and no stone over their heads. They lament and they cry in anger over this abysmal deed: six million children of Israel, the kin of David and the kin of Jesus, burned like foul flesh of dead sheep or dead camels!

TRUTH

Truth has no place in ethics, only living benevolence. Truth can easily be made to serve evil as well as goodness. The despots of the past and present seem to have had no difficulty in arraying before them defenders of their misdeeds with enough rationalization by truth to make their blackest strokes appear white. The truth walks on stilts of argumentation. Like the sirens of Odysseus, it will make an appeal to you sounding like heavenly sweetness and when you follow it, you will drown in hate and bitterness. The tyrants, small and huge, keep truths as handy weapons of persuasion. It is difficult to combat what they send forth *pro paganos* with other truths, those closer to your heart or any heart.

No truth is an answer; goodness is. Truth may be sometimes on the side of benevolence; kindness always is.

UNIFIERS

Stalin unified all the Russias. While he was at it he also unified Latvia, Lithuania, Estonia, and a dozen other small neighboring countries with Russia. Mao Tse-tung, the unifier of China with Tibet, is bent on unifying all of Indochina with Greater China.

"Unification" is a prettier name than invasion or conquest or genocide. The Romans, too, were masters of unification.

UNTOUCHABLES

Harijan, or "Children of God," is one of the gentler bynames for India's eighty-five million Untouchables, who are by mere birth reduced to a life of lowliest occupation at the lowest wage in a ghetto atmosphere that has no equivalent elsewhere.

The Untouchables of India, constituting one sixth of the population of this subcontinent, are a living example of the common phenomenon of our time: coexistence of ethical religion's traditional imagination and the most brutal practices in daily life. Hinduism, whether Vedic, Brahmanic, or sectarian, for millennia has given the black tribes of ancient India the stamp of the pariah, the stamp of the outcast.

All other castes—the four major ones and the myriad splinter sects—have appropriated to themselves the wealth of the land, the perquisites of the professions, and the profits from trade. For the blacks and poverty-dirty, the ruling classes reserved a range of work assignments from grave digging to garbage collecting. Today in the era of the great Gandhi's pitiful successors, this great body of seventy million pariahs must bring along their own dishes into restaurants, must dwell in slum ghettos on the edge of town, may not use public fountains. They may not even enter the home as servants except for cleaning septic tanks or latrines. So deeply are the Hindus infected by their religious prejudices against the black pariahs that in many regions a mere fleeting contact with an Untouchable requires an involved purification process. In many regions of India the pariahs may not walk barefoot on the sidewalk, may not pass a public well lest their shadow pollute the water, may not ride horseback, may not raise any cattle— only pigs and donkeys, symbols of dirt. When the blacks touch a caste person, they may receive a severe lashing.

Yet the Hindus involve themselves from childhood on in refined theologies of reincarnation of the purified soul; in dedication to Ahimsa, calling for non-violence to man or beast; in strict vegetarianism, blood being as abhorrent as flesh; in various degrees of sexual abstinence and celibacy; in reaching the state of Nirvana in which, cleansed of all desires, one lives in a perennial state of bliss.

The role of Hinduism in India is perhaps the most persuasive evidence of how a people can inherit, and carry on as a system, a sublime web of theological word play and ritual games, yet likewise maintain the brutal suppression of a black minority in their midst that they have cruelly relegated to the cesspool of the nation.

Perhaps the Hindus' religious duplicity can open the eyes of other religionists who say, Love thy enemy, yet cannot tolerate their next-door neighbor.

UTOPIA

Utopists since Plato's days have vied with each other in detailing their delectable futures; as the ancient carp said to the young fry swarming around the appealing tidbits— "Watch out for the hook."

The first, though visionary, plan for a state based on principles of ethical conduct aimed at the elimination of injustices, civic and otherwise, while also endeavoring to ameliorate human misery caused by human folly or oppressive tendency, was called *Utopia*. The author of this epochal work, Sir Thomas More, himself fell victim to despotism, but left a heritage of far-reaching consequence. Thomas More opened new vistas of ethical political thinking inspiring the great social reformers from Spinoza and Rousseau to Saint-Simon, Fourier, Owen and Proudhon.

Earlier utopias such as the Republic of Plato fell woefully short of an ethical goal; Plato and his epigone Aristotle were apologists for slavery and protagonists of an oligarchy by the aristocrats. Indeed, they bitingly attacked speakers for the equality of all men and races as "Sophists" trying to confuse black and white. Though contemporary Utopists project a heavenly equality, they too may be elitist.

VALUE

To discover what a man really values, watch his hands, not his lips. Man learned early to speak rapidly and earnestly of the lofty values he aspires to, while his hands reach out for the things he really desires. That applies equally to the dominant as well as the dominated.

The demagogue in politics never tires of exciting the imagination and emotions of his audience with fervent assurances about the benevolent concern whose pacific and humanitarian glow illuminates and directs his every purpose, while on both hands he carries the red mark of malevolent oppression. Who fails to recall the hoarse pitiful voice of Hitler crying out for a quiet niche in the world, a little place in the sun for peace-loving Germany? Who fails to recall the studied calm of Stalin in the tunic of an ordinary worker explaining with meeting-hall simplicity the gentle aims of a People's Democracy? Who fails to recall the poetic outpourings of Mao Tse-tung, the philosophical mandarin of Peking, calling for the bloom of "a hundred flowers" in freedom? And these three somehow managed, like stage magicians, to entrance a thousand million people with their dream-values, while, behind stage, the ax was severing head after head in butchering four and a half thousand men, women and children in one day; Louis XIV proclaiming France's cultural mission to Europe and falling on his neighbor countries, north, west and south, with marauding armies, burning, butchering, raping, year after year in an endless wave of terror; Ferdinand the most horrid infernos of history.

We may recall other value pretensions in the past as well as the present: Charlemagne, first head of the Holy Roman Empire, promising the Love of Christ to the Saxons and

and Isabella, monarchs of Spain, carefully taking absolution from their respective confessors, Jimenez and Torquemada, and then setting out upon perhaps the most callous and self-contradictory quest of that sad era: to arrest, blackmail and finally eradicate with fire and ax every vestige of two great races in medieval Spain, the Jews and the Moors. Nine thousand Jews, whose whole property they confiscated, men, women and children were burned alive at the behest of these two monstrous regents who carried love on their lips and the very devil in their hearts, the devil of greed.

I could go on at great length enumerating the double face of axiology. Such is human nature: more often than not, despotic rulers and ambitious climbers would hide their real ideals, ugly as they are, and profess ardently the most esteemed values of that day and place.

The small man often falls under the spell of the demagogues and cherishes the monsters for what they speak, not what they are. People are intrigued by the pretentious display of their ancient and recent glamorous leaders and few are the wary who take the trouble to examine deeply the facts of old, the facts of new, in order to measure lip-values against deed-values.

The maxims, Love thy neighbor, Love thy enemy, were taken from the Old Testament to become an inherent part of the New. The precept of love is a most serious one in the Christian faith; indeed, the command to love your neighbor and your enemy is exegetically identified with Christianity. So far, so good. Love is pure Christian ethics. But is it really? Can it be? Ethics implies activity, not a mere *Weltanschauung*. Is love an ethical element?

The Preacher sermonizes: Love thy enemy. Is love a true value unit? To judge by experience, no. If love implies action of helpfulness, certainly not. Commonly, by usage and fact, the term love in the religious sense not only today but always has been an academic concept, worthless, meaningless, like a coin without face, and significant only as a token in certain faiths.

Taking a long look at the Western arena over the last two thousand years, when love was taken out of Hebrew wisdom literature and made the bed upon which the flower of Christianity was to grow, one answers decidedly, No. From its early inception, Christianity professed love while under Roman suppression; when Christianity under the pagan Caesar Constantine became "Rome," this Hebrew-born faith became as bellicose, worldly and sanguine as Rome under the bloody centuries of Caesars.

I do not wish to elaborate on the most discouraging misdeeds that occurred under the successors of the Hebrew Simon whom they call Saint Peter. But as the Church became dominant and even after it split into Byzantine, Roman, Protestant and sundry splinter groups, there was no love in the doings of the bishops and no blessing in the group of pretentious aristocrats using the Church as cover. What about all the religious wars, the wars of conquest with bishops involved on each side, with altars, crucifixes and incense carried by false priests into foreign lands to convert their inhabitants to Christ by lance and chains? What about the despots upheld in foul government by subservient clergy, by the most unspeakable tortures inflicted on dissidents and diffidents while monks mumbled prayers, with slavery and serfdom not only explained away and tolerated, but even practiced by landowning bishops? Where are the ethics to a love that burned the Virgin of Orleans? Where are the ethics to a love that crusaded across eastern Europe, pillaging and massacring Jews and Moslems and finally even Christians who resisted? Where are the ethics to a love that quartered desperate peasants fighting for freedom? Where are the ethics to a love that sent highwaymen like Cortez and Pizarro to rob Indians of their gold under the pretense of a loving conversion?

If love is an ethical element, religious love is purely observance, empty, inactive. Even in our own nation, the preachers of love in the South have for centuries not only defended but advocated the rights of enslavement of the blacks, as the English clergy justified the military enslavement of the Irish and the Russian clergy the perpetuation of serfdom.

The leaders in the great struggle for freedom, men like Thomas Jefferson and Benjamin Rush, Voltaire and Rousseau, the truly ethical banner-carriers—whatever their message was, it did not read love. Love is a dirty word if you hear it spoken at an *auto-da-fé*. And no word was more frequent and more audible at the burning of the great army of innocent than love. Two hundred thousand German ministers, deacons and church officials called blessings upon Hitler and justified in sermon after sermon, talk after talk, the necessity of obliterating a people, infant and grandmother alike, just because they were of the same blood as their Lord, Christ. And all ended their sad apologias with the call of "Love thy neighbor."

Goethe once said that where an idea is missing, often a word takes its place. Love is such a word. There is no idea there. Our preachers in the South say: "Love thy neighbor," but they themselves close their gates to their black neighbors. They close their schools and their theatres. And they close their eyes when a Negro is persecuted or even murdered. Such is the emptiness of the word love; religious love requires nothing of its parishioner but to profess it. Ethics is not a matter of profession like a religious dogma. It is a matter of action, of materializing truly accepted values. Love, it is sad to report, in the western world is not a truly accepted value, but merely a theological pretense. Already in ancient Hebrew allegories, there is a tale of a beggar whose face was terribly marred. This poor man rose before the assembly and cried out: "Speak not to me of love! Love me not, but do right by me!" The victims of a thousand years of inquisition wanted surely no more love, but justice; I can see the Moors kneeling before their victorious baptizers begging for justice, not love.

VANITY

Vanity is the strongest of all evils. Lust has its natural limitations; avarice can attain surfeit; but vanity is never satisfied.

VENGEANCE

Vengeance on the Jews unto the thousandth generation as espoused by the Christian churches is hardly the spirit of the gentle Jew Jesus. Yet this is the one and only Christian thema that has never been attacked or eliminated by any of the Christian denominations. Everything in the holy scriptures of the Christians has been disputed at one time or another by theologians of the faith except this one promulgation: *Pereat Judea.* The Jew remains condemned for the life of the Church as killer of God; no scriptural volume is used in any of the Christian churches that does not depict the Jew as killer of God.

The Catholic Church under the leadership of the blessed John XXIII did convene at the Vatican and did take up the issue of deicide; there was a lot of fine theology, but in the windup, not a single Christian synod, not a single one, troubled to remove the sinfully false accusations against the Jewish people as such, against my grandchildren and yet unborn great-grandchildren, out of the "biographical" chapter of the New Testament. Christian children of all denominations, Catholic and Protestant, continue to drink with their milk of faith the poison of Christian Jew-hate. The poison may lie dormant in the bloodstream and then at any time of history, erupt in blood lust. Millions of Jews were massacred by Christians, and by Christians only, in two thousand years because the spirit of the blessed Jew Jesus was and still is overwhelmed by the Church call for eternal vengeance.

VIRTUE

Virtue, closely regarded, is one of the most commonly used terms to characterize man's relationship to fellow man. A person can not be with or without virtue except in relation to another person, as a measure can not be large or small except in relation to another measure. These simple facts notwithstanding, dominant individuals and groups, despotic or otherwise, have since memory serves us attempted to lay down or legislate definite rules of conduct, attitude or professed beliefs that in themselves carry an alleged mark of virtue.

The three religious virtues, common not only to Christian protagonists, namely Faith, Love and Charity, throughout the Middle Ages in Europe as well as Asia dominated the field of morality and history knows how small the share of Love and Charity was in this triad of virtue. Experience of Faith came easy to the Christian and Moslem world; as to Love, the witch-burners, the Jew-killers, the heretic-hunters, the riotous Crusaders, the Albigense-excisers, the Huguenot-bleeders—all these engaged in a thousand large and small wars of loving conversion. They proved only the intensity of Faith, not Love as a virtue. Love was a camouflage of much cruder and more sordid feelings; indeed, it was a ready excuse to persecute the weak and innocent, even as the pretense of peace has so often in history been a camouflage for "defensive" aggression on the part of despotic rulers or movements. And as to Charity, we find little of that third religious virtue in the centuries before the era of Enlightenment.

The professors and practitioners of religious charity defended the horrible institution of slavery, beginning with Augustinus and ending with the religious leaders in our Southern states. The situation in the Moslem countries has not been different except that in some of them, for instance Saudi Arabia, slavery of the crudest kind is still rampant while the pretty love calls still echo from the minarets. The Hindu religion has at no time taken issue with slavery, although it too dwells on the importance of the three virtues: Faith, Love and Charity. At close look, it is evident that the three religious flowers of virtue are mere artificial abstractions with as little significance as the four Platonic definitions of virtue, namely: Wisdom, Courage, Temperance and Justice.

The identification of wisdom with virtue, a Socratic favorite, is on its face untenable. We have seen throughout history wise men concoct ghastly acts of violence—to mention a few of the renowned sages, Marcus Aurelius, author of a popular little book of clever sayings, relegated Christians and other slaves to the wild beasts in the arena and frequently enjoyed this pastime; Constantine the Great, who turned the Roman Empire into a Catholic state, murdered his own young son, his wife and a palaceful of friends; Justinian, the erudite codifier of law, scourged Arians, pagans, Jews and other disbelievers with relentless cruelty. No one can deny that Napoleon was wise. The cultural elite of Red China devoutly follow the leadership of a professional philosopher, Mao Tsetung. Wisdom is no virtue and the erudite, often as not, are more given to viciousness than the simple or even confused.

The center of hate in totalitarian countries was always the *aristoi,* not the farm hands. The men who had assisted despotism in the past were men of learning and often wisdom. Who can deny the wisdom of Seneca, righthand man of bloody Nero, or the wisdom of Aristotle, teacher and intimate friend of both Philip and his conquest-thirsty son Alexander? Wisdom is not virtue nor does it always side with virtue; as often as not it sides with evil, with oppression and exploitation.

The other cardinal Platonic virtue, Courage, is certainly a misnomer since men of vicious design are as frequently imbued with courage as the truly virtuous. The third Platonic virtue of Temperance is plausible but meaningless. A person can be temperate in the Aristotelian sense and always seek the right mean between two extremes. This may make for a placid and prolonged life but not a virtuous one. No one can deny that Hitler lived a temperate life; he neither drank nor smoked, would not partake of meat in his consideration of animals and was in his sexual life quite restrained. Yet this temperate monster massacred more innocents than anyone else in history. Many are the examples of temperate individuals whose conduct was ugly and heartless.

While Plato finally adds substance to his ethical quadrangle by including Justice, this coming from him must be taken cautiously, since what Plato considers Justice might again turn out to be a misnomer. For instance, Plato is a strong protagonist of hereditary aristocracy being given charge of both superior fields of virtue, government and warfare. The working masses, on farms or fishing boats, in mines or workshops, are forever doomed in his ideal state to lowly unprivileged status. What Plato actually intended to add as a cardinal virtue was "proper order," not "justice." He as well as his pupil Aristotle opposed as tricksters (Sophists) those men of their time who proclaimed that all men were born free and equal, not, as these philosophers argued, half helots and half free.

If virtue is none of these seven fundamental moralities, philosophical and theological, what then is virtue? There were men in antiquity, in the Middle Ages, and modern times who argued for virtue as a state of being free from desire. Even Spinoza leans toward such a point of view; he wrote a major work on how to become free of driving affectations. Many churches, Christian, Hindu, Buddhist and others, have prohibited their priests and others from engaging in sexual activities, while some permit them to cater to other senses with fancy food and drink; others, like the Moslems and Jews, approve sexual activities but frown on certain foods or drinks.

I doubt if adherence to any of those precepts enhances one's virtue. It is easy for the man of weak or no potency to practice sexual abstinence, while many have little appetite for elaborate dishes or drinks. To consider a person virtuous because his sexual appetite is weak or nonexistent is as inconsistent as damning a man of strong potency for his desire. Thus the impotent appear saints, and the potent of the species, sinners.

190

There is no sin in exercising one's sexual capacity within the bounds of good taste and proper society and certainly no virtue in suppressing it. The men who have preached celibacy were obsessed with a bottomless guilt feeling, the root of which escapes me, or they were sexually impotent and made a virtue of their debility. In any case, suppression of normal sexual activity can only lead to bed-staining, onanism, pederasty or other abnormalities. No one is benefited by a man cutting himself off from normal bodily functions—and some misguided men even went to the extent of self-castration.

Virtue lies not in what one does to himself or herself. Virtue lies in the long road where you act and react with fellow man. Sometimes the most consistent practitioner of what is commonly and wrongly called morality, the man who never misses a mass or a prayer in church, mosque or synagogue, may be the meanest and most vicious man in town. There is no absolution for the ill-minded and ill-doing except in changing their ways. No amount of self-negation in pleasures of the day or pleasures of the night will turn the evildoer into a virtuous person. What one does with his or her body is his or her own problem. One may live moderately and sanely or dissipate oneself in utter foolishness. Virtue lies only in one's relation to others, to one's community.

The evildoer, the blackhearted hater, the oppressor, the exploiter, or the race rioter is *never* virtuous, no matter how continent he may be or how ardent a religious ritualist. Virtue lies in kindness and generosity, not in sexual or religious sublimation. It is time that even the churches wake up to this fact, that you can not preach love inside the church and tolerate hate outside. It is not enough to serve God in Heaven; you must also serve man on earth.

WARS

Wars are like knives; they are a blessing in the hand of the surgeon, a scourge if possessed by the assassin. To be an absolute pacifist is to oppose even the struggle for freedom of the downtrodden and suppressed.

He who refuses to go to war against wanton cruelty is not peace-loving, but rather, indifferent. History shows that the determined fight only one war against the oppressor; the appeasers, many.

WITCHCRAFT

The horror and anguish in the ancient game of witch-craft was caused not by its practitioners but by its suppressors.

WITNESS

What did the witnesses say when Queen Isabella, King Ferdinand of Spain and the reigning pope ordered nine thousand Jews burned alive in the year following the discovery of America by Columbus? What did the millions of witnesses to this monstrous bestial pyre of quaking human flesh, the Christians of Europe, what did the onlooking believers in Lord Jesus say? Nothing.

What did the witnesses of Christian Europe say when the pope and his bishops inflamed Jerusalem-bent crusaders to march east and on the way stop in city after city to dip their swords in the blood of the Children of Israel, cutting down the unaware man, woman and child, sick and crippled? The Crusaders sang and yelled, Let's make an end of the

God-Killers here! The towns of France and Germany reverberated with the anguished cries of the innocent. What did the Christians of Europe say? Nothing!

When the Christian clergy ordered the kings and other rulers to put Jews to torture trial because of alleged well-poisoning, blood drinking, desecrating the Host, uttering profane sayings, what did the Christian witnesses say to all that unspeakable persecution? Nothing!

Even as the Christian people of Europe said nothing to the gassing of six million Hebrews by the Germans or the outrages committed by the Russians since Stalin. The voices of the Christians are silenced when Jewish blood is spilled; following the precept of Pope Pius XII, the Vatican is a neutral body. However, the great Christian organization did protest the despoiling by American troops of vegetables and fruits and brushland. Such doings offend the Lord, they claim.

WORDS

As a student attending school, you open the pages of your book and read, trusting that the authors of your books meant to inform you, to enlighten you, to help you. But when you leave your school for a brief period or for good, the books you come across, the journals or the speeches, the press, radio or any of the many other sources of communication—these lie in wait for your eye, ear and mind, traps set by public figures and agents who are dominated by a desire or purpose to misinform you, to confuse you, to destroy your loyalties and superimpose upon them a series of falsehoods and egotistical schemes. You have learned in years of study the wide scope of our traditional democracy, yet these wilful and sometimes naive agents of confusion will try to overwhelm you with false yet cunningly contrived charges against your own style of freedom and point to their own miserable lands of despotic oppression as heavens, as "People's Democracies."

Agents of lands run by self-perpetuating political cliques

193

or military dictators will brazenly charge your duly elected officials with being lackeys of "certain" ruling classes, while they themselves never hold true elections, indeed, offering to their subjects only one slate, the one appointed by the ruling camarilla. They will lie about your country and its leaders, hoping that a lie big enough and repeated often enough will be taken for truth by many, all too many. Such propaganda will reach you again and again! It is important that you learn early to expect it and look through its falsehoods. Words are cheap and the enemies of our country make abundant use of this cheap currency in voice and print.

They arm to the teeth and then propagandize you to refuse to bear or even assemble weapons. They conquer their neighbor countries and admonish you to refuse your government's call to help the attacked. Czechoslovakia, Tibet, Hungary, Korea, Poland, East Germany, Latvia, Estonia, Lithuania are only some of the nations overrun by the common enemy claiming to have been "threatened" by each of them. The enemy invariably hollers for peace when he is planning aggression. Hitler and Stalin used the word peace more often than any other public figures in Europe.

They will call your government "warmongering" to confuse the issue of their own conquest activities. They support subversion and treason in other countries with words as well as with weapons; if you don't watch out they will plant missiles at your very doorstep or a thousand miles away, be it Cuba or Cambodia.

Your country is a thorn in their side; your people's affluence makes them ill. They want you to share with them your wealth and they will share with you their poverty and misery.

They are colossal failures in economic and social achievement and nothing pleases them more than propagandizing you to follow their footsteps and thus bring your country to their level, down at the bottom; with two or three families in one apartment; with no right of any worker to strike at any time; with no right of anybody to speak his or her mind, or

194

to assemble in protest; with no religious freedom, no job freedom, with no rights over your own young child.

Our enemies do not wish to help us but rather to bury us. If they are so clever, why are they so poor? If they are so noble, why did they put a wall around their country? If they are so kind, why do their best citizens wind up in Siberia?

A word can break a man; no words can make a man!

WORSHIP

Do not kneel before God. He hardly welcomes subservience. Do not prostrate yourself before Him. He is not a potentate expecting kowtow. Beseech Him not with folded hands; He is no willful pasha of the desert. Just love Him; more yet, love His creatures and He will surely guess the rest. Treat God not like a Lord of the Manor; look at Him as the Lord of all Good Deeds and Good Endeavors. Stand upright and think upright. That is all there is to worship.

WRITERS

Writers are not mere people. They are messengers. Some write for kings and despots; others, for schemers and dictators. Their messages may be clever but foul. Good writers are often not good people. Caesar was his own writer; Nero, the last of that line, kept a stable of them. Some write for their pocket. Money is their bag. Others yearn for accolades and serve the sirens of fame or infamy. They are sisters in repute and repute is money, ill or good, they both carry reward in their bosom.

For these writers, the Dollar Sign serves as weathervane. When the wind blows sexward, they will pen a topless tale; when they are bewildered by space physics, they fabulate about Marsmen and monsters on Venus or Jupiter; when mobs are in motion, itched on by political Mafia from the Left or the Right, they mix it up for whatever it's worth. They are the pharmacists of the pen; they write according to prescription; they write for money. There are ugly names for those who make love for money. Has anyone got a good name for those who pander literature for money?

There is money in politics and more money in Red politics than any other kind. Hoods make riots, and next year become lecturers at frightened universities, commanding more cash for an appearance than they could get for working a year. Gamy accusations imbedded in a thick paste of four-letter words are gobbled up by the gullible. The clowning radicals have learned that by using revolting words they can sound like revolutionaries. When they have made it to the platform of public repute, they fly to different pastures, in the Red colonies where the pay is steady.

YOUTH

Youth is such a happy era because the sun of promise is still high in the sky.

Youth is given to all, yet so very few of the young make the romance of that era live on throughout their life. The drabness and banality of daily realism surrounds, infiltrates, and finally punctures the lofty dream world of youth.

Blessed the dreamer, mature and awake, who has the gift of holding on to the visions of youth! What a poor substitute is reality for the world of imagination and hope!

So many of those who today talk of "youth" ignore the fact that there is no such thing. There are many "youths." There is American youth; there is Russian youth, Chinese youth, African youth, Argentine youth. And in every country there is more than one "youth." Each group has its own aspirations, its own ideologies, different from the others. American youth may not want to go to war; Russian youth eagerly volunteers to go to war against Israel, which is as far from them as Cambodia is from the United States.

So all this talk about "youth" is no more than superficial generalization. The world of the young is as unable as the adults to get along with its counterparts in the other lands.

Age in itself does not imply wisdom, but neither does youth. So many identify adolescence with novel path-breaking ideology. Nothing could be further from the truth. Turning your back to the past does not necessarily open vistas to a better tomorrow. At all stages of history, positive elements existed in man and his social structure. It appears, however, that the essential elements of true humanitarianism have more often than not succumbed to obvious negativism. Law turned into oppression, social movements into sanguine bureaucracies, sermons of love into boring and often even horrid religious ritualism that in its clamor for acceptance would incarcerate, starve, beat and even burn the flesh to force a soul to obedience.

If youth is the bearer of a new era, how come nowhere in Russia or Poland where three million gallows are waiting for the rest of Europe's Jewry, is a single voice raised among the young to end the scourge of anti-Semitism? Indeed, the Young Communist League of Russia charges that the Jews plan to conquer the globe from their den in Zion. If youth is the hope of the day, how come they recite the sayings of Mao with fervor in great China, the young people's republic where not a single Jew may reside and where slogans appear: Israel is the Taiwan of the Mediterranean; Drive the Jews into the Mediterranean! Further south, in the subcontinent of India where the youth will not eat flesh or drink fermented fruit, to them the Israelites do not exist at all. They want no ambassador or delegates from God's Chosen Sufferers. The Hindus of India softly chant prayers on the Ganges and berate loudly the Israelites on the East River of New York.

The Romans who were the first to defend the right of the Jew to his religion (*religio licita*) considered the treatment of the Jews as a touchstone of civilization. Glancing at two-thirds of the world's youth, I have serious misgivings at what blessings we can expect from them. They are rather loudly proclaiming a new era; all I hear is the same vocalization of hate and harassment.

Perhaps we should turn to the tranquility of the aged. *Ex senectute lux:* from age, the Light. Perhaps the youth will learn from the experience of the old that the old hates have brought no blessings and that noise is a poor substitute for understanding.

Old age does not slow us down; it is youth that speeds us up, often recklessly. It is easier to hasten without being burdened by knowledge or experience. Is it better thus? I doubt it.

ZEALOTS

Zealots are responsible for more killings than sinners. Remember the Inquisition, the Crusades, Nazism, Communism.

ZEITGEIST

I have sown the seeds of betterment
 for all my living years;
I wonder where the missives went
 and did they reach my peers?
Why is life's pattern so confined
 to surface and success,
Why do the castles higher climb
 while crumbles fundament?
The greed of greeds, the wars for might—
 will hate here never end?
The time is short, the pace is slow;
 half life is squandered on the start;
And then the years are fleeting by
 with all afraid to miss the chance
To fill their dreambag
 With golden dreams;
And soon the reaper will be here
 And end the play for you and me.
Oft have I pondered if I made
 A dent on time, a dent on man or child
To lead a better life,
 of generous beginning,
A life of courage to reject

The despots, right or left,
A life of God the Spirit and the Giver,
Not God in service to some church;
But God unbound and unencumbered
By hate or prejudice
A God to love by deeds
Not hollow hymns and vows.

ZIONISM

Zionism, or the feeling of togetherness with the people of Israel, is the essence of Judaism. The Hebrew faith again and again declares its indomitable determination to return to the land of divine promise and to overcome all efforts of hostile subjugation. If religion means binding, this sublime devotion is the heart and soul of the Hebrews. Any effort like that of Soviet Russia and its satellites to deprive the Jews of Zionism is merely a calculated attempt to destroy the Jews' heritage, to destroy the Jews' tomorrow. As the National Socialists of Germany endeavored to destroy the Jew's body, the Russian Communists endeavor to destroy the Jew's soul.

I wish I could return a thousand years hence and find out if the ancient Hebrew was right—that there will always be with us the stench of Satan, that nothing new can come to this world.

200